NEW HAMPSHIRE

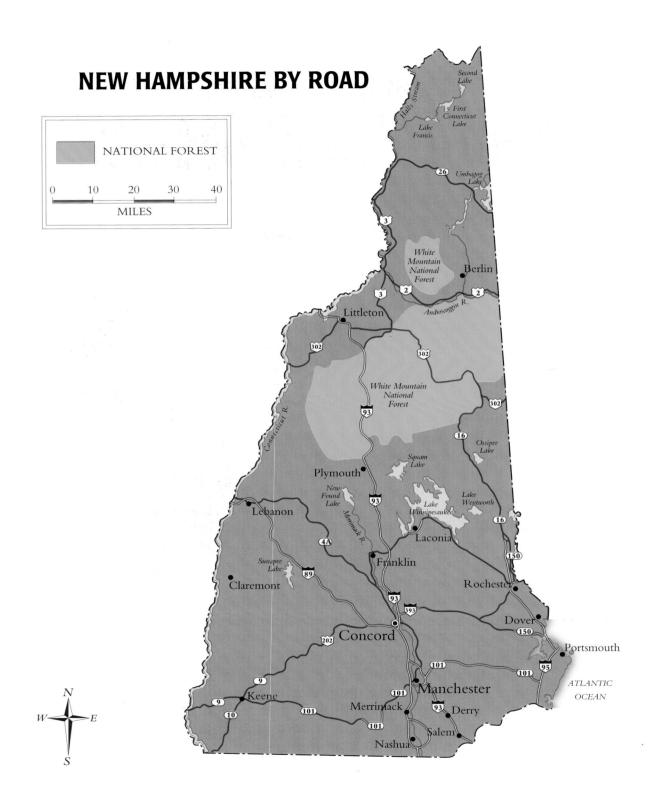

NEW HAMPSHIRE BY ROAD

NATIONAL FOREST

0   10   20   30   40
MILES

N
W   E
S

Halls Stream

Second Lake

First Connecticut Lake

Lake Francis

Umbagog Lake

26

3

White Mountain National Forest

Berlin

3   2

2

Androscoggin R.

Littleton

302

302

302

White Mountain National Forest

93

16

Ossipee Lake

Squam Lake

Connecticut R.

Plymouth

New Found Lake

93

Lake Wentworth

Lebanon

Lake Winnipesaukee

16

4A

Merrimack R.

Laconia

150

Sunapee Lake

Franklin

89

Claremont

93

Rochester

393

Dover

150

202

Concord

Portsmouth

101

95

9

101

101

ATLANTIC OCEAN

Keene

9

101

Manchester

101

10

Merrimack

101

93

Derry

Salem

Nashua

CELEBRATE THE STATES
NEW HAMPSHIRE

Steve Otfinoski

BENCHMARK BOOKS

MARSHALL CAVENDISH
NEW YORK

Benchmark Books
Marshall Cavendish Corporation
99 White Plains Road
Tarrytown, New York 10591-9001

Library of Congress Cataloging-in-Publication Data
Otfinoski, Steve.
New Hampshire / Steve Otfinoski.
p.   cm.——(Celebrate the states)
Includes bibliographical references and index.
Summary: Surveys the geographic features, history, government, economy, people,
and landmarks of New Hampshire, one of the six New England states.
ISBN 0-7614-0669-7 (lib. bdg.)
1. New Hampshire——Juvenile literature. [1. New Hampshire.] I. Title. II. Series.
F34.3.O84   1999   974.2——dc21   97-50379   CIP   AC

Maps and graphics supplied by Oxford Cartographers, Oxford, England

Photo research by Candlepants Incorporated

Cover photo: The Picture Cube / John Yurka

The photographs in this book are used by permission and through the courtesy of: *William H. Johnson*: 6-7,
20-21, 61, 66-67, 69, 71, 76, 79, 100-101, 105, 107, 117, 126. *The Image Bank*: Walter Bibikow, 10-11; Steve
Dunwell, 16, 108; Pete Turner, 22; David Brownell, 59; Michael Melford, 65; Joe Devenney, 112; Ulf Wallin,
113. *The Picture Cube*: Walter Bibikow, 14, 110; Frank Siteman, 17, 128; Glenn Kulbako, 18; Andre Jenny, 46-
47, 135; Rick Scott, 54, 116; Greig Cranna, 58; Eric A. Roth, 62; Tom McCarthy, 73; John Coletti, 75, 85;
Jeffery Dunn, 80; Bob Kramer, 114; Steve Solum, 119(right); Ralph Reinhold, 123; Robert Baldwin, back
cover. *Photo Researchers, Inc.*: Tim Davis, 23; Farrell Grehan, 52; George Ranalli, 78; Lawrence Migdale, 109;
Stephen Krasemann, 119(left); Rod Plank, 122; *New Hampshire Historical Society*: 26-27, 29, 33, 36, 37, 87,
90, 129(left), 129(right), 130. *Archive Photos*: 31, 35, 93. *Jay Michaels/SAGA/ Archive Photos*: 132. *Manchester
Historical Association*: 39. *Piscataqua History Club Collection, Portsmouth Athenium*: 43. *Paul Avis*: 44. *Office of
the Governor*: 50. *Razz Berry Photo*: 55. *Stephen Avery*: 70. *Kent Hanson*: 82. *Corbis-Bettmann*: 89, 91, 94.
© 1998 *Suki Coughlin*: 98. *Office of the Secretary of State*: 118(lower).

Printed in Italy

3 5 6 4 2

CONTENTS

NEW HAMPSHIRE IS...

New Hampshire is a beautiful state . . .

"This is the second greatest show on earth."

> —showman P. T. Barnum admiring the view from
> atop Mount Washington

. . . with memorable landmarks . . .

"It seemed as if an enormous giant or titan had sculptured his own likeness on the precipice. There was the broad arch of the forehead, a hundred feet in height, the nose, with its long bridge; and the vast lips, which, if they could have spoken, would have rolled their thunder accents from one end of the valley to the other."

> —newspaper account of the Old Man of the Mountain

. . . and determined people.

"'Yes,' said Dan'l Webster. 'I've got about seventy-five other things to do and the Missouri Compromise to straighten out, but I'll take on your case. For if two New Hampshiremen aren't a match for the devil, we might as well give the country back to the Indians.'"

> —Stephen Vincent Benét in his story
> "The Devil and Daniel Webster"

"I'm proud to be a resident of a state that best exemplifies so many of the legendary characteristics of the mystical New Englander, even those not always considered by some to be attractive. I'm speaking of frugality, fierce independence, shrewd business sense, ingenuity—and not a little pride."

> —Judson D. Hale Sr., editor-in-chief of *Yankee* magazine

New Hampshire attracts artists and writers . . .

"They [visitors] may go to Vermont for repose, but they come to New Hampshire for inspiration."

—Jim McIntosh, travel writer

"Nearly half of my poems must actually have been written in New Hampshire. . . . Four of my children were born in Derry, New Hampshire. . . . So you see it has been New Hampshire with me all the way. You will find my poems show it, I think."

—poet Robert Frost, 1938

. . . and every four years, a host of politicians.

"We're so passionate about our primary. We believe we're one of the last places where, without spending a fortune, you can establish yourself as a viable candidate for President of the United States."

—Donna Sytek, Speaker of the New Hampshire House of Representatives

---

The old and the new come together in New Hampshire. It is one of the nation's oldest states. It is also one of the most modern—home to a thriving high-tech industry. It is a place of great natural beauty, inhabited by a proud and independent people. Come meet New Hampshire.

1 THE LAY OF THE LAND

The geography of New Hampshire has a larger-than-life quality to it. What other state has as its emblem a man's face carved by nature out of rock? Or can boast of a range of lofty mountain peaks named after United States presidents? (The highest, of course, is Mount Washington.)

History and fiction come together in the rugged, grand landscape of this New England state. Its countryside has attracted writers, artists, and poets for generations. From the White Mountains to the sandy beaches of its tiny coastline, New Hampshire is a delight for natives and tourists alike.

MOUNTAINS, NOTCHES, LAKES, AND RIVERS

New Hampshire is one of the six New England states. Its neighbor to the west is Vermont. The two states fit snugly against one another like two pieces of a jigsaw puzzle. To the east lie Maine and the Atlantic Ocean; to the north, Canada; and to the south, Massachusetts.

Writer Dennis Fradin described New Hampshire as "a slice of pie that wasn't cut straight." It also resembles a key, broad at the bottom and narrow at the top with one side flat and the other notched.

New Hampshire is the seventh-smallest state, but within its borders is a great variety of landforms. In the southeast, New

LAND AND WATER

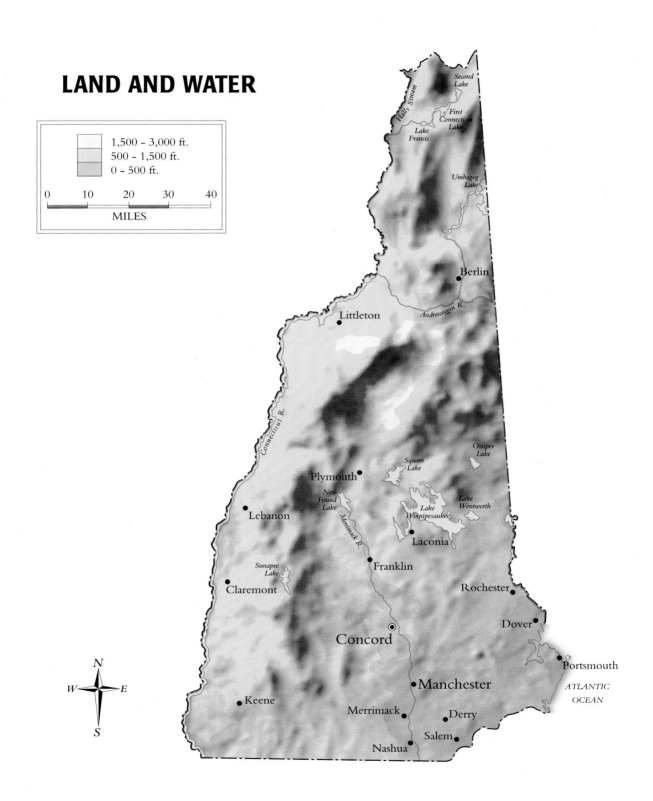

	1,500 – 3,000 ft.
	500 – 1,500 ft.
	0 – 500 ft.

0   10   20   30   40
MILES

Second Lake

First Connecticut Lake

Hall's Stream

Lake Francis

Umbagog Lake

Berlin

Androscoggin R.

Littleton

Connecticut R.

Ossipee Lake

Squam Lake

Plymouth

New Found Lake

Lake Winnipesaukee

Lake Wentworth

Laconia

Lebanon

Merrimack R.

Sunapee Lake

Franklin

Claremont

Rochester

Dover

Concord

Portsmouth

ATLANTIC OCEAN

Manchester

N
W   E
S

Keene

Merrimack

Derry

Salem

Nashua

Tourists admire the rocky coastline of Star Island, one of the four islands owned by New Hampshire in the Isles of Shoals.

Hampshire has eighteen miles of coastline on the Atlantic Ocean. It is the shortest coastline of any state that borders an ocean, but New Hampshire has made good use of it. The coast is studded with beaches that attract thousands of sun worshippers each summer. Hampton Beach, with its colorful amusement park, is the biggest. Six miles offshore are the Isles of Shoals, named for the shoals, or schools of fish, that swim nearby. Four of the islands are owned by New Hampshire and the remaining five belong to Maine. These rocky isles were inhabited for generations by fishermen and their families. Appledore Island is home to the Shoals Marine Laboratory, a laboratory and summer school operated by the University of New Hampshire and Cornell University.

The New England Uplands are north of the coast and cover roughly the southern half of the state. Through here run the two most important rivers in New Hampshire—the Connecticut River, which divides it from Vermont, and the Merrimack River. The Merrimack, which flows through the center of the state, provided energy for many industrial mills in the 1800s. The small cities of Concord, Manchester, and Nashua grew up along its banks. North of the Merrimack, before the mountains begin, lies a region of lakes. The biggest of these is Lake Winnipesaukee.

Most of the northern half of the state is dominated by the White Mountains, named for their bald, chalk-colored peaks. The greatest peaks are in the Presidential Range. Individual peaks are named for Presidents Adams, Jefferson, Madison, and Monroe. All of these are more than a mile high. Towering above them all is Mount Washington. At 6,288 feet, it is the highest peak in the Northeast.

Far smaller, but just as fascinating, are New Hampshire's five monadnocks. These are age-old rocks that are so hard they didn't wear down as the rest of the surrounding land was eaten away by erosion over countless centuries. The most famous is Mount Monadnock in the southwest. It was a favorite hiking spot for the nineteenth-century authors Nathaniel Hawthorne, Herman Melville, and Ralph Waldo Emerson. Today, over 125,000 visitors

A bridge spans the Connecticut River, which divides New Hampshire from Vermont.

MOUNT WASHINGTON

"All my life I have admired and felt in awe of Mount Washington," says travel writer Skip Sheffield. Many New Hampshirites would agree with him. Not only is it the highest point in the Northeast, but it also has a proud history. The Algonquin Indians considered Mount Washington a sacred place. Early white settlers established hiking trails in the 1700s, some of which still exist. In 1869, a coal-fired, steam-powered cog railway was built to run to the summit. It is the oldest continuously run railway of its kind and has the second-steepest track grade in the world.

If you don't trust the train and don't feel like hiking, you can drive a car up the mountain. But don't try it from October to May because the road is closed. During this time Mount Washington has some of the roughest weather anywhere on Earth, with high winds and an average of fifteen feet of snow through the winter. It actually snows at the summit eight or nine months out of the year.

"I see more weather pass me in a week than most meteorologists see in a long time," boasts one staffer at the mountain's weather observatory. All in all, Mount Washington is one memorable mountain.

make the climb to the top of the 3,165-foot-high mountain each year. Few mountains on Earth have more climbers. "It's not so much a wilderness experience as it is a social happening," says ranger Ben Haubrich.

Another famous landmark is the Old Man of the Mountain, a face that nature has carved into the rock. This amazing natural formation stands forty feet high and looks over Franconia Notch, one of eight notches, or natural breaks, in the White Mountains.

A pair of hikers pause to take in the magnificent view from atop Mount Monadnock.

THE DEVIL'S FOOTPRINT

Every natural formation in New Hampshire seems to have some legend or piece of folklore to explain it. Take the Devil's Footprint, a formation near Milford. The story goes that the Devil invited the men in the neighborhood to a baked-bean dinner. He cooked the beans in a big pothole amid the rocks, probably planning to trap the men after they ate. While he was dishing out dinner, the Devil stepped on a rock made soft by the heat from his cooking. He couldn't get his foot free and started roaring in frustration. The men were frightened by the sound and fled, unwittingly saving their souls. The Devil finally managed to get his foot out, but his footprint remains in the rock still. Or so the legend goes.

There's an Old Woman of the Notch too, who is less famous than her husband but has the added glamour of hair, formed by trees and brush.

CLIMATE

New Hampshire is generally cool in the summer and very cool in the winter. "The winters are way too long and the summers are too brief," complains nurse Roxi Toews, who lives in West Swanzey. "We grieve the end of summer." But many other people who enjoy winter sports celebrate the coming of winter. The White Mountains receive an average of one hundred inches of snow a season and are a magnet for skiers.

Spring is brief, but a welcome relief after the long winter. Fall is brisk and chilly and filled with the beauty of the autumn leaves and

their brilliant colors. Thousands of southern New Englanders and New Yorkers make a yearly pilgrimage to see the leaves of New Hampshire, which doesn't please some natives. "It's a spectacular time of year, there's no doubt about it," says one crusty North Conway resident. "But the [Mount Washington] Valley absolutely comes to a standstill because of the crush of people trying to get through."

Worse than the tourists are the blinding snowstorms called blizzards that sometimes paralyze the state. Although blizzards are the most common natural disaster in New Hampshire, few are as

Boys enjoy a game of ice hockey on frozen Lake Winnipesaukee, New Hampshire's largest lake.

well remembered as the hurricane that struck the state in September 1938. Most hurricanes that come up the Atlantic coast never make it as far north as New Hampshire, but this one did. Half of the state's white pines were destroyed, and winds at Mount Washington topped 180 miles per hour.

BIG TREES, WILD ANIMALS

Forests cover about four-fifths of New Hampshire. The only state with a greater percentage of forestland is neighboring Maine. Ash,

White Mountains National Forest is ablaze with color every fall.

beech, elm, fir, maple, oak, and pine trees abound. The distinctive white birch is the state tree. In the shadow of the big trees flourish such flowering shrubs as mountain laurel and rhododendron. Wildflowers are a joyful surprise to hikers on forest trails and include black-eyed Susans, goldenrod, violets, and the state flower, purple lilac.

Small animals thrive in New Hampshire's fields and forests. There are large populations of rabbits, foxes, raccoons, beavers, porcupines, and, hold your nose, skunks. Squirrels and chipmunks can be seen amid autumn's fallen leaves, gathering nuts and seeds for the long New Hampshire winter. Game birds such as ducks and pheasants roam the woods and wetlands and make the state a

This squirrel isn't sure it wants to get any closer to the striped skunk—for good reason! These are just two of the many wild animals that roam the state.

DEALING WITH THE DEER

Deer are one of the most common wild animals in New Hampshire. Some people see this as a blessing, others as a curse. As suburbs spread out into once rural land, deer are appearing in many people's backyards, eating every plant in sight. In some places the situation has grown out of control. The state banned deer hunting on Long Island, a two-square-mile island in Lake Winnipesaukee, in 1970. Twenty-five years later the deer population had nearly tripled. The deer had eaten almost every shred of greenery and were starving.

The state sent in a sharpshooter from Connecticut who killed two-thirds of the herd in three nights. The killing was quick and the deer meat, called venison, was distributed to homeless shelters throughout the state. Animal lovers and environmentalists condemned the killing. The island's residents breathed a sigh of relief. Both sides continue to debate the thorny issue of how to prevent the deer from taking over again. One solution has been to reinstate the fall hunting season.

hunter's paradise. Deer have made a comeback in New Hampshire over the past few decades. And so have black bears and moose.

The number of coyotes has been steadily growing in New Hampshire. Today, probably more than six thousand of them live in the state. "I would wager there's not a town anywhere in New Hampshire that doesn't have resident coyotes," says wildlife biologist Kent Gustafson. "It's not unusual for anybody in the state to hear them yipping and yapping and howling." These wild creatures pose little threat to humans, but attack and eat their pets, especially cats.

POLLUTION PROBLEMS

New Hampshire has taken good care of its natural environment. In recent years, it has had the best record in the nation in reducing the poisonous gases and chemicals released by factories and power plants. It has cut 87 percent of all air pollution since 1987. The state's industries and utilities are among the cleanest-burning in the country.

But that doesn't mean the state is pollution-free. Far from it. The culprits are not in New Hampshire but in upwind states as far away as the Midwest. In particular, the pollution from these states' coal-burning utilities has an unpleasant habit of drifting over New Hampshire and other New England states. This pollution creates dangerous chemicals that are brought to the ground by precipitation. This is called acid rain. Acid rain has polluted the state's waterways, killing fish and other marine life. It has killed trees in New Hampshire's forests, curling leaves and poisoning their root systems. "The good news is that acid rain isn't getting worse," reports scientist Bruce Hill of the Appalachian Mountain Club in Gorham. "The bad news is, it may not be getting better, at least, not fast enough."

This may soon change. In 1997, the Environmental Protection Agency passed stricter air pollution standards in twenty-two states, including several in the Midwest. If they don't reduce pollution levels by over a third by the year 2007, these states could lose some federal funding. New Hampshire isn't one of the states, but it could benefit greatly from the reduction in pollution.

2 A PROUD PAST

Crawford Notch, by Thomas Hill

"Live Free or Die" is New Hampshire's state motto. Its people are so proud of it they even display it on their license plates for everyone to see. The motto is attributed to John Stark, the state's greatest general of the American Revolution. Freedom has been important to New Hampshirites since the first settlers arrived in 1623—freedom from Indian attacks, from Great Britain, from the overbearing federal government.

While some people have sacrificed their lives to defend New Hampshire's freedom, many more have found a reason to live in a state where independent thinking and action are highly valued.

THE FIRST INHABITANTS

In the beginning, there were the Indians. Native Americans probably arrived in present-day New Hampshire about 12,000 years ago, as the last huge ice sheets called glaciers began to retreat from the region. Indian artifacts, dating back some 9,000 years, have been unearthed near Lake Winnipesaukee.

By the time Europeans arrived in the region, most of the area's Native Americans belonged to the Algonquian-speaking family of tribes. They farmed in the summer, growing corn, beans, and squash. In the winter they hunted deer, moose, and other animals. They lived in small villages of huts called wigwams. To make

The Indians of New Hampshire adapted well to their environment. Here they play a ball game on the winter ice.

wigwams they formed oval domes by tying poles together. They then covered the domes with bark or animal skins. Although New Hampshire's Indians got along well with each other, they learned to fight in order to defend themselves from their sworn enemy, the Iroquois, who lived in what is now upper New York State.

EARLY EXPLORATION

The first Europeans to explore what is now New Hampshire may have been Vikings from northern Europe. Some experts believe carvings on a boulder outside of Hampton were made by a Viking explorer in about A.D.1100.

Italian explorer Giovanni da Verrazano may have gotten a glimpse of the White Mountains from his ship on the Atlantic in 1524. Frenchman Samuel de Champlain was one of the first Europeans to explore the region. He sailed into the mouth of the Piscataqua River in 1605.

However, it was that wily Englishman Captain John Smith who was the greatest booster for New Hampshire. After his adventures in Virginia, where he helped found Jamestown, the first permanent English colony in North America, Smith sailed the seacoast of New England in 1614 and landed in the Isles of Shoals. He named them Smith's Isles after himself.

Returning to England, Smith wrote a book about his travels, *Description of New England*, in which he praised New Hampshire: "Here should be no hard landlord to rack us with high rents . . . here every man may be master and owner of his labor and land in a short time." Such promising prose tempted many an Englishman to risk the long ocean voyage and begin a new life in New England.

THE THIRD COLONY

New Hampshire became the third English colony to be settled, after Virginia and Plymouth. In 1622, King James I gave a large tract of

In 1614, John Smith sailed the New England coast and landed in the Isles of Shoals. He called the waters near the isles "the strangest fish-pond I ever saw."

land in New England to Sir Ferdinando Gorges and John Mason. In 1629, the two men divided their land. Mason's land was bounded by the Merrimack and Piscataqua Rivers. He named it New Hampshire, after his native English county of Hampshire. Gorges's land, lying east of the Piscataqua River, later became Maine.

The four original settlements in New Hampshire are often referred to as the Four Towns—Dover, Portsmouth, Exeter, and Hampton. A fifth settlement, at Odiorne's Point, was founded in 1623 but did not survive. Dover, first called Hilton's Point, was established by Edward Hilton on the Piscataqua River the same year. Colonists representing Mason settled on a hillside covered with wild strawberries in 1630. They called it Strawbery Banke.

Today, it is the thriving city of Portsmouth. Exeter was founded on land sold to the Reverend John Wheelwright by the Squamscott Indians in 1638. Colonists from Massachusetts founded Hampton the same year.

By 1640, the Four Towns had about a thousand people. Hardly enough, they felt, to sustain a colony. The following year they joined the Massachusetts Bay Colony for protection. Yet, being New Hampshirites, they basically continued to govern themselves. They made their livelihood from lumbering in New Hampshire's rich forests, fishing from its waters, farming the land, and trading furs. By the 1650s, a thriving shipbuilding industry developed in Portsmouth, which possessed an excellent harbor.

In 1679, the English King, Charles II, separated New Hampshire from Massachusetts and made it a royal colony. The two colonies were rejoined in 1689 and then separated again in 1692.

THE FRENCH AND INDIAN WARS

When the first European settlers had arrived in New Hampshire in the 1620s, the Indians welcomed them. In 1644, Passaconaway, a great Pennacook chief, made a peace treaty with the settlers. The peace of Passaconaway lasted until the 1670s. Then, colonial growth, slow but steady, came to be seen by the Native Americans as a threat. War eventually broke out and would continue for nearly a hundred years. At first, the Indians fought the settlers by themselves. Then they formed an alliance with the French, who wanted to drive the British from North America.

The French and Indian Wars started with a bloody bang when a

MAN OF PEACE

He was New Hampshire's first great Native American leader. Passaconaway, whose name means "Child of the Bear," was chief of the Pennacook Confederacy, a group of Indian bands living along the Merrimack River. About halfway through his long life, he saw the first English settlers arrive in his land. Passaconaway decided the only way to deal with these newcomers was to make peace with them. "I commune with the Great Spirit," he told his people in a famous speech before his death. "He whispers me now—'Tell your people. Peace, Peace, is the only hope of your race.'"

When Passaconaway died in 1665, the legend goes, a pack of wolves pulled his body on a sled to the peak of Mount Washington, where sled, wolves, and body all vanished in a cloud of fire.

band of warriors descended on the town of Dover in 1689. The attack was an act of revenge. Thirteen years earlier in Dover, several hundred Indians had been captured through trickery and sold into slavery. The man who helped set the trap was a dishonest trader, Major Richard Waldron. During the raid, the Indians forced Waldron to sit in a chair. Then each brave slashed Waldron's chest with a knife, crying, "See! I cross out my account." As the wars dragged on, atrocities continued to be committed by both colonists and Indians.

THE AMERICAN REVOLUTION

The French and Indian Wars finally ended in 1763 with England driving the French out of North America. But the colonists were unhappy when England imposed heavy taxes in order to pay its large war debts. Eventually dissatisfaction led to revolution.

New Hampshire was the only one of the original thirteen colonies where no full-fledged battle of the American Revolution was fought. Still, one of the first military actions of the war, before Lexington and Concord, took place in New Castle, New Hampshire. John Sullivan, a New Hampshire lawyer and politician, led a group of patriots in seizing military supplies from a British fort in 1774.

Moreover, New Hampshirites made up for their lack of action on the home front by participating in the fighting elsewhere. New Hampshire volunteers outnumbered the combined soldiers from Massachusetts and Connecticut at the Battle of Bunker Hill. George Washington himself claimed New Hampshire soldiers were "far superior to the other colonies" in their "bravery and resolution."

John Sullivan was one of New Hampshire's Revolutionary War heroes. He was also a lawyer and a delegate to the First and Second Continental Congresses and was twice elected governor of his state.

Portsmouth, a center of New England shipbuilding, turned out three ships for the Continental navy, including the *Raleigh*, which was captained by naval hero John Paul Jones. About one hundred privateers operated out of Portsmouth. These vessels harassed British ships and stole their cargo and supplies. New Hampshire's General John Stark led the American troops to one of their first and greatest victories over the British at the Battle of Bennington in Vermont in 1777.

Connecticut is known as the Constitution State because in 1639 it adopted the world's first written constitution, but New Hampshire could lay just as much claim to that title. On January 5, 1776, it

General John Stark leads American soldiers to victory at the Battle of Bennington in Vermont. As a young man, Stark was captured by Indians and adopted into their tribe.

became the first colony to adopt its own temporary constitution and create a government independent of England. The delegates to the Constitutional Convention of 1787 decided that when nine states ratified, or formally approved, the Constitution, it would take effect. On June 21, 1788, New Hampshire became the decisive ninth state to ratify the document. As a part of the new United States, New Hampshire first established its capital in Portsmouth. In 1808 the capital was moved to Concord, where it has remained since.

A COUNTRY WITHIN A STATE

In 1832, New Hampshire was the scene of one of the strangest episodes in American history. The narrow northern tip of the state had been in dispute between the United States and Canada since 1783. Tired of the controversy, the people of this 250-square-mile region declared themselves independent of both countries. They called themselves the Indian Stream Republic, after a stream running through the territory. For the next few years they remained an autonomous nation, with their own constitution, legislative assembly, and forty-man militia. By 1836, the "republic" conceded it was a part of New Hampshire, and the Webster-Ashburton Treaty of 1842 officially

The busy port city of Portsmouth in the mid–eighteenth century, the first state capital of New Hampshire

established the border between the United States and Canada. The Indian Stream Republic was no more.

WAR AND INDUSTRY

By the early nineteenth century, slavery was becoming a controversial issue dividing the South, which depended on slave labor, from the North, where slavery was less common. In 1835, Congressman John Dickson of Keene became the first person to speak out against slavery in the United States Congress. New Hampshire had many stops along the Underground Railroad, a system of escape routes for runaway slaves fleeing north from the Southern slave states and toward Canada, where slavery was illegal.

The struggle over slavery finally led to the Southern states seceding from the Union early in 1861. Within a few months, the Civil War began. An estimated 35,000 New Hampshire men answered the Union's call and fought in the Civil War. Nearly 5,000 of them died.

After the North won the war, an industrial revolution swept through the East. New machines could produce clothing and other products much faster than the human hand could. Factories and mills sprang up across the Northeast. Immigrants, many of them from France and Canada, flocked to New Hampshire to work in the mills.

The largest and one of the oldest of the state's many textile factories was in Amoskeag. It had been established in 1809 along the Merrimack River in Manchester. In 1837, the company bought a 15,000-acre tract along a canal and built a self-sufficient

This view of the Amoskeag Millyard dates to about 1840. Generations of European immigrants worked and lived at the mills, including the Irish, Germans, Swedes, and French Canadians.

industrial town where employees both worked and lived. By the early 1900s, Amoskeag was the largest textile manufacturer in the world, employing 17,000 men, women, and children. Thomas Smith began working at Amoskeag as a child of fourteen in the early 1900s. He recalled working in the hot, dirty mills:

THE OLD GRANITE STATE

The Singing Hutchinson Family of New Hampshire wrote and performed their antislavery songs from the 1840s through the Civil War. This was their theme song, and they opened every concert with it.

By Jesse Hutchinson

mu - sic, With a band of mu - sic we are pass - ing 'round the world.

We are all real Yankees,	Liberty is our motto,
We are all real Yankees,	Liberty is our motto,
We are all real Yankees,	Liberty is our motto,
From the Old Granite State.	In the Old Granite State.
And by prudent guessing,	We despise oppression,
And by prudent guessing,	We despise oppression,
And by prudent guessing,	We despise oppression,
We shall whittle through the world. *Chorus*	And we cannot be enslaved. *Chorus*

Yes, we're friends of Emancipation,
And we'll sing the Proclamation
Till it echoes through our nation
From the Old Granite State.
That the tribe of Jesse,
That the tribe of Jesse,
That the tribe of Jesse,
Are the friends of equal rights. *Chorus*

The hardest job I had in the mills was . . . cleaning out the picker machines. All the cotton seeds that came out of the cotton would drop down under the pickers, and we would have to go under there and get all those seeds. We'd have a wad of cotton in our mouth to filter out the dust and keep us from choking. It would be so hot, and we'd get that cotton seed on our skin, and it would hurt you something terrible.

Following World War I, Amoskeag fell on hard times due to stiff competition from newer mills in the South. By 1935, most of the company's mills were shut down for good.

DEPRESSION AND ANOTHER WAR

The 1930s were hard times for people throughout the state. Economic depression cost many their jobs. Terrible floods in 1936 and a hurricane in 1938 cost some people their very lives. The United States' entrance into World War II in 1941 put thousands back to work in Portsmouth shipyards repairing warships and building submarines. Even the textile mills returned to life, turning out military uniforms for soldiers. Sixty thousand New Hampshirites served in the armed forces during the war.

But even in the midst of war New Hampshire was in the forefront of making peace. In July 1944, representatives of forty-four nations met at Bretton Woods in the White Mountains to form the International Monetary Fund and the World Bank. These organizations were intended to promote free trade when the war ended and help countries rebuild themselves through international loans.

The submarine Redfish *is christened in January 1944 at Portsmouth, which was a major shipbuilding center during World War II.*

MODERN TIMES

The postwar years saw New Hampshire growing, as towns spread out and absorbed neighboring rural communities as suburbs. In 1963 the state came up with a novel way to raise money for public education. They instituted the first legal lottery in the United States

High-tech manufacturing is a very important industry in New Hampshire today.

since the end of the 1800s. Since then, lotteries have become a common way for states to raise revenue.

In the 1970s, the growth of the electronics industry brought new wealth and prosperity to southern New Hampshire. High-tech companies have found it an attractive location both because it is near the big city of Boston, Massachusetts, and because it has neither a sales tax nor a state income tax.

New Hampshire today is a far cry from the agricultural state it once was. But the spirit of the state's founders is still very much alive. "Live Free or Die" is more than a motto on a license plate. It speaks for a people who value their independence above almost anything else.

3 THE DEMOCRATIC WAY

The capitol in Concord

Politically, New Hampshire is a study in contradictions. A refuge of bedrock Republicanism for decades, in 1996 it elected a woman Democrat as governor. Its house of representatives has more members than that of any other state, but each legislator is paid only one hundred dollars a year. It has no state income tax and no general sales tax, but its property taxes are among the highest in the nation. On one thing, however, nearly all New Hampshirites will agree. They insist on having a say in how their government is run— New Hampshire has one of the most stubbornly democratic governments in the United States, if not the world.

INSIDE GOVERNMENT

New Hampshire's government, like every state's, is divided into three branches: executive, legislative, and judicial.

Executive. The chief executive officer of New Hampshire is the governor. The governor appoints officials to state government, prepares the state budget, and recommends programs to the legislature. New Hampshire is the only state besides Vermont where the governor's term of office is only two years, not four. There is also no office of lieutenant governor in the state. Instead, New Hampshire has an executive council made up of five members. This council is a holdover from colonial times, when a royal council oversaw the

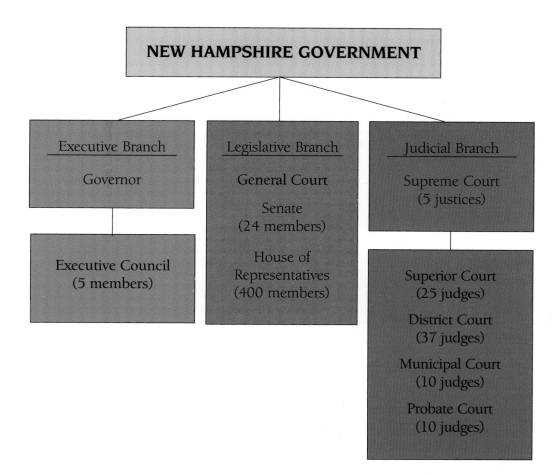

NEW HAMPSHIRE GOVERNMENT

Executive Branch

Governor

Executive Council
(5 members)

Legislative Branch

General Court

Senate
(24 members)

House of
Representatives
(400 members)

Judicial Branch

Supreme Court
(5 justices)

Superior Court
(25 judges)

District Court
(37 judges)

Municipal Court
(10 judges)

Probate Court
(10 judges)

governor's actions. Council members are elected to two-year terms and advise the governor on important issues. They also approve all major appointments the governor makes.

From 1857 through the early 1960s, nearly all New Hampshire's governors were Republican. But it wasn't always that way. Before 1850, the state voted staunchly Democratic. The Republican Party was started as an antislavery party, which gave it strong appeal in liberal New Hampshire. As the state grew in population, it became more conservative. So did the Republican Party.

Governor Jeanne Shaheen is the state's first woman governor. "I think I got elected because I addressed issues that make a difference for the average family—improving the schools, lowering electric rates, affordable health care," she has said.

Since the 1970s, New Hampshire has become more politically balanced, as more Democrats have been elected to state offices. In 1997, Democrat Jeanne Shaheen became New Hampshire's first woman governor. "We are here to serve the people of New Hampshire," Governor Shaheen said in her inaugural address. "They are not interested in whether we are Republicans or Democrats, liberals or conservatives, men or women. What they expect from us is results, or at least an honest effort to achieve them."

Although she was more liberal than many of her predecessors,

Governor Shaheen's emphasis on family concerns and education appealed to the people of New Hampshire.

Legislative. The New Hampshire legislature, which is called the General Court, has two houses—a twenty-four-member senate and a four hundred–member house of representatives. The only larger legislative body in the entire country is the U.S. House of Representatives itself.

Because New Hampshire's legislators earn only two hundred dollars for a two-year term, they usually hold down full-time jobs in addition to their government duties. Along with making new laws, the state legislature passes the state budget and can propose amendments to the state constitution.

Judicial. The highest court in New Hampshire is the state supreme court, which has a chief justice and four associate justices. The supreme court evaluates whether laws or cases violate the constitution and whether cases from lower courts were handled correctly. New Hampshire also has a state superior court, probate courts, municipal courts, and district courts. All judges in the state are appointed by the governor and serve until they turn seventy, when they must retire.

In 1990, David Souter, a state supreme court justice, was appointed to the U.S. Supreme Court. Souter was born in Massachusetts but moved to a farm in Weare, New Hampshire, with his family when he was eleven. Because of his longtime connections with conservative Republicans, many people expected Souter to almost always uphold conservative positions. He has surprised them, however, by becoming an open-minded moderate on the Court.

221 LITTLE REPUBLICS

State government is only half the story in New Hampshire. Self-government is so much a part of New Hampshire's communities that the state's 221 towns are often referred to as "little republics." The voters in every town elect their own officials and approve how tax money is spent.

The foundation of self-government and the purest form of

The residents of Sandwich, New Hampshire, have their say on local issues at the annual town meeting.

democracy in New Hampshire is the town meeting. Held once a year, the town meeting allows each citizen eighteen years of age or older to speak out on public issues and then vote as a group to pass ordinances, make town improvements, elect local officials, and deal with other business. "On town-meeting day . . . I would sit on the benches in the back of the town hall after school," Supreme Court justice David Souter recalls, "and that's where I began my lessons in practical government."

A TAX HAVEN

New Hampshire is one of the few states that has no state income tax or general sales tax. No wonder so many businesses, big and small, have flocked there. If there is one issue most New Hampshirites can agree on, it is no more taxes. In other states politicians promise not to raise taxes but often do once they are elected. But in New Hampshire they are duty-bound to stick to their word. In the early 1970s, arch conservative William Loeb, the publisher of the *Manchester Union Leader*, New Hampshire's biggest newspaper, came up with "the pledge." The pledge is a promise made by every person running for public office not to raise existing taxes or support new ones, especially an income tax or a sales tax. Even liberal Democrats have taken the pledge.

But revenue must be raised somehow to pay for education and other public services. There are taxes on such products as alcohol, tobacco, and gasoline. Restaurant meals and hotel rooms are also taxed. So is property. Property taxes in New Hampshire doubled in just four years during the 1990s, angering many homeowners.

THE PRIMARY STATE

Every four years for about a month the entire nation turns its attention to New Hampshire. The New Hampshire primary is the first, and many believe the most important, presidential primary. It was held for the first time in 1920. Since 1952 it has accurately picked the winner of the presidential elections every time but once.

The New Hampshire primary has made national figures of politicians like Eugene McCarthy, George McGovern, and Gary Hart. It ended the presidential aspirations of another, Edmund Muskie, when he supposedly cried in public over accusations against his wife made by a local newspaper. When George Bush won the presidency in 1988 he closed his speech with the words "Thank you, New Hampshire."

The New Hampshire primary is so important that in 1997 a library and archives devoted to the primary's history opened in Concord. The library, the first of its kind in the nation, includes in its collection everything from books to campaign buttons. Terry Shumaker, a member of the library's board of trustees, says, "The New Hampshire primary is a unique institution."

Not all of New Hampshire's children begin school with kindergarten. It is the only state that currently does not offer public kindergarten for all five-year-olds.

THE KINDERGARTEN CONTROVERSY

Having low taxes means that New Hampshire doesn't always have the money to fund programs common in other states. One issue that arises again and again is kindergarten. New Hampshire is the only state that currently does not have public kindergarten for all five-year-olds. About 30 percent of the state's school districts don't offer kindergarten. This is upsetting for many residents, especially those who have moved to New Hampshire from other states.

The Sutcliffs moved to Hudson, New Hampshire, from Wyoming and now pay to send their five-year-old son to a private kindergarten. "We budget our house, our car," says Paige Sutcliff. "We didn't budget kindergarten." She and another mother have started a campaign to pressure state lawmakers to pay for public kindergarten statewide.

Proposals have been floated to help communities start kindergartens with money from an increase in the cigarette tax. But many conservatives object. "We're opposed to the cigarette tax because we're opposed to tax increases, period," explains Roy Stewart, chairman of a group called the Granite State Taxpayers.

Because education is paid for primarily by property taxes, many New Hampshirites feel they are already paying enough for schooling. "Kindergarten is not the government's responsibility. It's parental responsibility," says state representative Bob Clegg. "The parents I've talked to in my community have said they want to keep their kids home. How do you tell them they need to pay for public kindergarten?"

Many educators argue that kindergarten is essential to the development of good students and citizens. "Kids at age five learn faster than kids at age six, and it slows down after that," claims state education consultant and early education expert Helen Schotanus.

The struggle between those New Hampshirites who want more social services and those who want to keep taxes low will undoubtedly continue. In 1997, Governor Shaheen approved a program promising state aid to those communities that want to have kindergartens. But the program did not specify where the money was going to come from. The day when New Hampshire has universal kindergarten may still be a long way off.

THE ECONOMY

In fifty years, New Hampshire has grown from a state of small farms and midsize factories to become the nation's fourth most industrialized state. After a rough stretch in the early 1990s when it suffered an economic recession, New Hampshire's economy has bounced back.

New Hampshire is known as the Granite State, and this hard rock from the state's quarries has been used in many famous structures, including the Library of Congress in the nation's capital. But the state has few other valuable minerals, so mining remains a minor industry in New Hampshire.

GROSS STATE PRODUCT: $41.2 BILLION

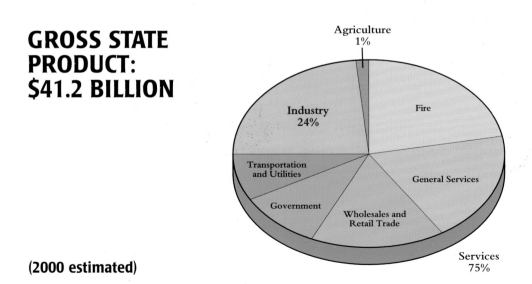

Agriculture
1%

Industry
24%

Fire

Transportation
and Utilities

General Services

Government

Wholesales and
Retail Trade

Services
75%

(2000 estimated)

Logs arrive by truck at a mill to be ground into wood pulp.

A much more plentiful natural resource is timber. About 85 percent of the state is covered with forest, so the lumber industry is
important here. Cedar, pine, spruce, and other softwood trees are
turned into paper and pulp. Hardwoods like ash, birch, and oak
are used for lumber and other wood products. New Hampshire fir
trees grace many a northeastern home during the holiday season.
One of the most popular products to come from trees is the rich,
thick syrup from the maple. The sap from the trees runs in late win-

"Everybody helps out come sappin' time," says maple sugar farmer Tom Hunter. "We're still using spouts and buckets instead of plastic tubing. And we boil with wood, not oil. I think you can taste the difference."

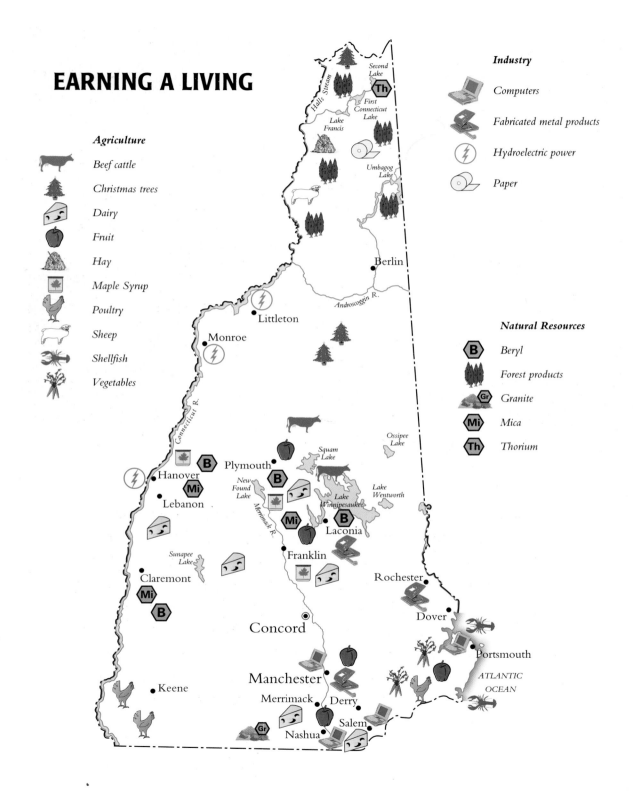

EARNING A LIVING

Agriculture

- Beef cattle
- Christmas trees
- Dairy
- Fruit
- Hay
- Maple Syrup
- Poultry
- Sheep
- Shellfish
- Vegetables

Industry

- Computers
- Fabricated metal products
- Hydroelectric power
- Paper

Natural Resources

- B Beryl
- Forest products
- Gr Granite
- Mi Mica
- Th Thorium

Second Lake
First Connecticut Lake
Halls Stream
Lake Francis
Umbagog Lake
Berlin
Androscoggin R.
Littleton
Monroe
Connecticut R.
Hanover
Mi
Lebanon
Plymouth
Squam Lake
New Found Lake
Merrimack R.
Mi
Franklin
Laconia
Lake Winnipesaukee
Lake Wentworth
Ossipee Lake
Sunapee Lake
Claremont
Mi
B
Rochester
Dover
Concord
Keene
Manchester
Merrimack
Derry
Nashua
Gr
Salem
Portsmouth
ATLANTIC OCEAN

Visitors to the Smith Farm in Laconia pick their own strawberries.

ter and is tapped through mid-April. Maple syrup, maple sugar, and other maple products are gobbled up by natives and tourists alike.

Today, agriculture accounts for only about 1 percent of New Hampshire's gross state product. Fewer than two thousand farms remain. Many of those that have survived are devoted to dairy products, especially milk and eggs. Vegetable farms produce large quantities of sweet corn and potatoes. Fruits such as apples, blueberries, and strawberries grow well in New Hampshire's short growing season. Beef cattle and sheep are also raised in the state.

A lobsterman prepares a trap near Seabrook. Commercial fishing is a small but steady business in the state.

Fishing on New Hampshire's short coast has always been a thriving, if modest, business. Cod, haddock, and flounder are among the fish caught commercially in these waters. Shellfish like shrimp and lobster also abound.

Inland, fish farming became popular in the 1990s, as the number of fish in the oceans diminished. In ponds and tanks across the state, entrepreneurs raise such fish as flounder, salmon, and trout. Fish farming has its advantages. "Compared to cows and sheep, they never get out in the middle of the night and stand in the middle of the road," says Debbie Gile, a trout farmer, who previously tried raising livestock. "Nobody ever calls and says, 'Your fish are out.'"

The real backbone of the state's economy is industry. New Hampshire factories turn out everything from machine tools and radio and television equipment to farm machinery and shoes. The first shoe factory was established in Weare in 1823. Today, New Hampshire is one of the nation's leading leather manufacturing states.

In the 1980s, many high-tech companies, especially those producing computer parts, moved into southern New Hampshire, lured by the state's low taxes. New Hampshire's lovely countryside also attracts business. The city of Portsmouth, for example, has recently experienced a building bonanza with two new hotels and the expansion of a third. Patrick Ford, president of National Hotel Realty Advisors, says, "You come for business, and you get an opportunity to get around a little bit, you fall in love with the area."

NOUVELLE HAMPSHIRE

New Hampshire is no longer entirely a land of quiet towns and quaint country lanes. They still exist, but a new New Hampshire is crowding out the old one. A writer for the *Washington Post* has called this modern-day state "Nouvelle Hampshire" and the name has stuck.

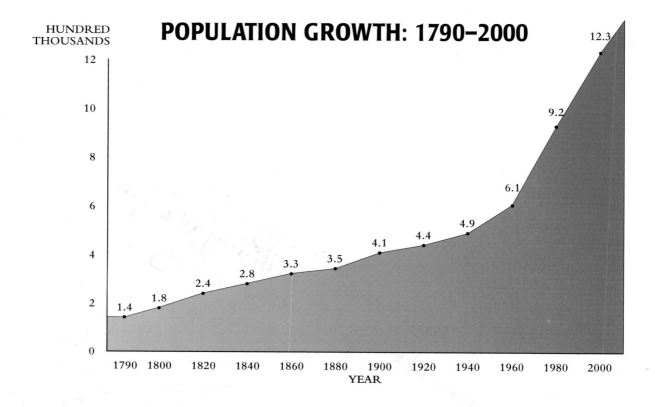

POPULATION GROWTH: 1790–2000

HUNDRED THOUSANDS

YEAR

1.4   1.8   2.4   2.8   3.3   3.5   4.1   4.4   4.9   6.1   9.2   12.3

This "new New Hampshire" is inhabited by entrepreneurs who have moved there to open companies and make money. They have been followed by real estate developers who have replaced the old downtowns with shopping centers and new housing developments. Even Manchester's old Amoskeag Mills have been converted into office space.

Some people are concerned that an influx of new residents will bring new problems that New Hampshire hasn't had to deal with much before—problems like crime, poverty, drugs, and other social ills common in states with large urban populations.

Whatever problems come with prosperity, New Hampshire cannot look back. In the past, Yankee ingenuity has helped it solve problems and adapt to changing times. It must continue to do so in the future.

The covered bridge in Stark is a quaint reminder of simpler times.

NATIVES AND TRANSPLANTS

4

From its mountains to its seacoast, New Hampshire's landscape is filled with variety. The state's people are far more uniform. Ninety-eight percent of the population is white. About one percent is Hispanic. The remaining one percent are either black, Native American, or Asian. The largest ethnic group is French Canadian. Many French Canadians came here in the nineteenth century to work in the mills and factories. They have kept much of their culture, their French language, and their religion, Roman Catholicism. Parts of northern New Hampshire have so many French Canadians that visitors may forget they are still in the United States.

A NICE PLACE TO LIVE

If you're looking for a good place to live and raise a family, New Hampshire is the place for you. In the whole state there are only slightly over a million people, about the same population as the city of San Diego, California. There are no crowded cities or urban slums, and New Hampshire has one of the lowest violent crime rates in the nation. "People here are a lot more down to earth than in other places," says writer Michael Schuman of Keene. "The lifestyle is relaxed. But where I live you're also only two or three hours from Boston and New York City."

These factors, combined with the natural beauty of the country-

Sleigh rides at a Christmas tree farm are just one of the activities enjoyed by New Hampshirites.

side, have made New Hampshire an attractive place to live for many people. In June 1997, *Money* magazine ranked three of the state's cities—Nashua, Portsmouth, and Manchester—in the top ten best places to live in the United States. Nashua was number one. "The kids raised here want to live here when they grow up," says Nashua mayor Donald Davidson. "Great public schools, a revitalized economy, positive attitudes—we offer a better life for everybody. We're much more conscious of preserving what we have."

THE HIGHLAND GAMES

Did you ever toss a caber? Play a clarsach? Wear the tartan of your clan?

If you're Scots, you know a caber is a huge pole thrown in athletic contests, a clarsach is a Scottish harp, and tartan is a woolen cloth woven with the particular design of your Highland family group, or clan. If you're not Scots, you might still enjoy all these things at the New Hampshire Highland Games, held every September at Loon Mountain in Lincoln.

Each year, 35,000 people attend this three-day festival of Scottish culture. Scotch-Irish immigrants were among the earliest European settlers in New Hampshire, and the games give their descendants a chance to celebrate their rich traditions. Besides contests, feats of strength, and music (don't miss the bagpipe bands), there are representatives of sixty Scottish clans ready to help visitors learn about their heritage and clan.

Dartmouth is New Hampshire's most distinguished college.

EDUCATION

New Hampshire has always been concerned about the education of its children. The one-room school was an institution in colonial times and some are still standing today, although they are no longer used. The first public high school in the nation was founded in Portsmouth in 1830, and the first free public library supported by tax dollars opened in Peterborough in 1833.

New Hampshire is home to Dartmouth College, an elite Ivy

League school and one of the ten oldest universities in the country. Dartmouth began as Moor's Indian Charity School, which was founded by the Reverend Eleazer Wheelock in Connecticut in 1754 as a school for Native Americans. In 1770, he moved the school to Hanover, New Hampshire, and renamed it Dartmouth College. Colonial governor John Wentworth wanted to attend the first graduation and had a sixty-seven-mile road built through the wilderness so he could get there. One wonders if the governor was disappointed on his arrival—Dartmouth's first graduating class numbered four men! Today Dartmouth is among the nation's best schools with one of the largest college libraries in the nation.

As good as it is, the New Hampshire educational system does have its problems. Since nearly all money for education is raised through property taxes, residents of poor school districts complain that their schools have less money to spend and are inferior to those in richer districts. Some schools are so underfunded that they have had to cut music and art classes and some sports just to have enough money to buy textbooks. Franklin High School is one of the worst in the state, with poorly paid teachers and classrooms that are literally falling apart.

When Franklin senior John Costella played a basketball game at nearby Bow High he was overwhelmed by how great the school looked. "They have computers in every class," he said. "I'm telling you, if I went to school there, every day I would kiss the floor." Bow, needless to say, is a much richer town than Franklin.

In December 1997, the state supreme court ruled that New Hampshire's system for funding education was unconstitutional. It said a fairer way had to be found to fund schools statewide. The

Education has been on the mind of many New Hampshirites in recent years.

court gave state legislators a year to set new standards and find a way to pay for them. The most obvious way is to create a state income tax. Thomas Connair, a lawyer in Claremont, hailed the decision as "a courageous statement that the status quo in 'Live Free or Die' politics is unconstitutional."

State senator James Rubens doesn't see it that way. For him the decision is "the most abrupt and radical change to state and local government in this century." He believes that New Hampshire should change its state constitution to avoid complying with the decision. No matter what happens, the issue of adequately funding schools is not going away.

RELIGION

For many years, most New Hampshirites were Protestant. The Congregational Church, the church of the Puritans, was the established church in each town. Until 1819, everyone was required to pay a tax to support the minister. Today, more residents are Roman Catholic than Protestant.

Church attendance, however, is not what it once was. The beauty of nature and year-round outdoor activities do not make for faithful churchgoers, believes Reverend Brad Bergfalk, the pastor of a church in Concord. "Nature becomes a substitute for traditional religious expression," he says.

There were very few Jewish people in New Hampshire until the early 1900s. The Shapiro House in Portsmouth's Strawbery Banke Museum was once the home of Russian Jew Abraham Shapiro and his family, who settled there in the early 1900s. Visitors to the museum can learn about the home life of one of New Hampshire's Jewish immigrant families. Sharon Kotok, a museum employee, says the exhibit "explodes the myth that all of these old New England locations were then populated only by descendants of the *Mayflower*."

THE OUTDOORS

When not working, the people of New Hampshire like to play. In the summer they enjoy hiking and mountain climbing. A group of adventurous hikers call themselves the 4,000 Club. Each of them has climbed all thirteen peaks in the White Mountains that top four thousand feet. Hiker Dan Tetreault of Center Conway and a friend have actually climbed all thirteen peaks in one day. They called it the Death March. "We ran into some other hikers up there," says Tetreault. "When we told them our plan, one guy said, 'You'll never make it in a day.' We snickered. Far from discouraging us, it put a spring in our step." By the end of the day, they were exhausted and barely able to keep going. When they finally made it to the top of Mount Webster, "I had a huge feeling of accomplishment and a big, goofy grin that didn't go away for days," Tetreault recalled. "It may have been called the Death March, but I've never felt so alive in my life."

New Hampshire is a skier's paradise.

Others seeking less challenging recreation enjoy swimming and sunbathing at the crowded beaches on the state's coastline or at the resorts along Lake Winnipesaukee.

Winter is for skiing, sledding, and ice skating. All of these sports are part of the state's winter carnivals. One of the oldest and most popular winter carnivals is held at Dartmouth College in February. Snow sculpture is a favorite activity at the carnival. Groups of college students work tirelessly for days to create their colossal snow figures, some soaring as high as thirty feet.

Sports enthusiasts flock to the auto race held each July in Loudon. The race is three hundred laps long, a little over 317 miles, and has never been won twice by the same driver.

Autumn is the time when thousands of "leaf peepers" from all over the country arrive in New Hampshire. "The colors of the leaves exploded and were aflame everywhere I looked," Jeff Smith, a chef who is better known as the Frugal Gourmet, once wrote about a trip to Lancaster. "The white of the birch trees formed the canvas on which the colors were displayed and I was calmed. . . . I swear I could smell the history of the colonies right in the air."

HONORING THE PAST

The state's history can also be smelled, seen, and tasted at its country fairs, a harvest tradition for generations, where you can

Giant snow sculptures make the Dartmouth Winter Carnival one of the most popular in New England.

Autumn scenery brings thousands of tourists, or "leaf peepers," to New Hampshire every fall.

enjoy such time-honored events as vegetable and livestock contests, games and rides on the midway, and dazzling nighttime fireworks displays.

Some New Hampshirites are so fascinated by their history that they bring it to life every chance they get. They stage re-enactments of famous battles from colonial times. In July 1997, hundreds of history buffs gathered to re-enact a siege by the French and their Indian allies at Charlestown, once the northernmost English outpost on the Connecticut River. The participants, who work regular jobs weekdays, dressed as English soldiers, French marines, and Indian warriors. If the French hadn't lost the siege, the course of history may have been very different and northern New England and Canada may have remained in French hands for many years.

"These re-enactors take their roles less as a weekend hobby than a constant sub-theme in their lives," writes journalist Keith

Morris Dancers perform at a country fair in Canterbury.

PUMPKIN MILK SHAKES

Pumpkin has been a favorite vegetable in New Hampshire since Indian times. Most everyone has eaten pumpkin pie or roasted pumpkin seeds. But a pumpkin milk shake? Don't knock it till you've tried it.

½ pint vanilla ice cream
¼ cup milk
½ teaspoon vanilla extract
4 tablespoons canned pumpkin
nutmeg
yellow and red food coloring

1. Mix the ice cream, milk, and vanilla extract in a blender.
2. Add the pumpkin and sprinkle in a dash of nutmeg for flavor.
3. Add a drop or two of the food colorings to make your shake orange.
4. Now drink and enjoy!

Henderson. "Nearly every summer weekend is given to making history come alive."

AN ARTISTS' HAVEN

Creative people have always been drawn to New Hampshire, with its dramatic landscapes and live-and-let-live natives. Nathaniel Hawthorne was one of them. His story "The Great Stone Face," about the Old Man of the Mountain, made it one of the most celebrated natural landmarks in the country. Poets such as Joyce Kilmer and Robert Frost have also found inspiration in the New Hamp-

ETHNIC NEW HAMPSHIRE

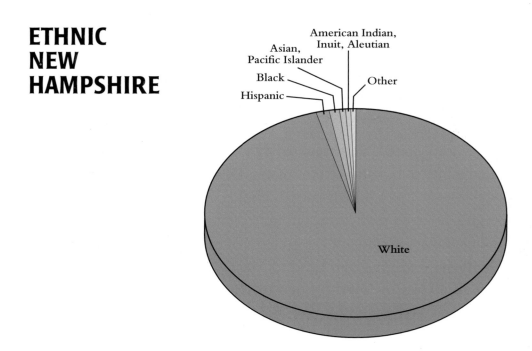

The MacDowell Colony is a peaceful retreat for composers and other artists.

shire landscape. Artist Maxfield Parrish was so taken with New Hampshire that he moved permanently to Plainfield. The mountain peak of Ascutney, which Parrish could see from the window of his studio, appears many times in his fanciful illustrations.

But the artist who left the greatest mark in the state was perhaps composer and musician Edward MacDowell, who moved with his wife to a farm in Peterborough in 1896. After his death in 1908, his widow completed his plan for the MacDowell Colony, a haven for writers, composers, and artists.

At this retreat, creative people can get away from the hustle and bustle of the outside world and devote themselves to their work. Only one day a year—usually in August—are the grounds open to visitors. On that day, the MacDowell Award is presented to an outstanding artist, writer, composer, architect, or filmmaker. Among the famous Americans who have sought the solitude of the MacDowell Colony are writer Thornton Wilder and composer Aaron Copland.

Although they don't get invited to the MacDowell Colony, some of New Hampshire's most creative people have been inventors. Hair clippers, the machine lathe, and the hacksaw were all invented by New Hampshirites. Elias Howe hailed from Massachusetts, but he did some of his best work on his invention, the sewing machine, while staying in Nashua.

Then there is Thaddeus Lowe, who was born in Coos County. He built a balloon in 1861 and flew it more than five hundred miles, from Cincinnati, Ohio, to near Unionville, South Carolina. President Abraham Lincoln was so impressed with the possibility of using balloons for spying that he made Lowe chief of the Corps of Aeronautics of the U.S. Army. During the Civil War, Lowe successfully launched a fleet of observation balloons that allowed a view behind Confederate army lines. After the war, Lowe continued to tinker, eventually inventing, among other things, the first ice-making machine.

Whatever brings people to New Hampshire—scenery, sports, or the freedom to create—they invariably fall in love with the Granite State.

5 NOTABLE NEW HAMPSHIRITES

"New Hampshire's historical heroes are, for the most part, somewhat flawed or, worse, erroneously credited to Vermont," writes Judson D. Hale Sr., editor-in-chief of *Yankee* magazine. While the careers of some notable New Hampshirites took them far from their home state, they all displayed a strength of character typical of people from the Granite State.

THE SADDEST PRESIDENT

From the beginning, Franklin Pierce, New Hampshire's only native son to become president, seemed destined for great things. He was born in 1804 in a log cabin at Hillsboro Lower Village. His father fought in the Revolutionary War and was later twice elected governor of New Hampshire. Young Franklin had dark good looks that earned him the nickname "Handsome Frank." He studied at Bowdoin College where he met classmate Nathaniel Hawthorne, who would become one of America's greatest authors and Pierce's lifelong friend.

Pierce soon entered politics. He was an impressive speaker and was elected to the state legislature, then to the U.S. House of Representatives and finally to the U.S. Senate. He might never have become president if the Democratic convention nominating the presidential candidate in 1852 was not deadlocked between four

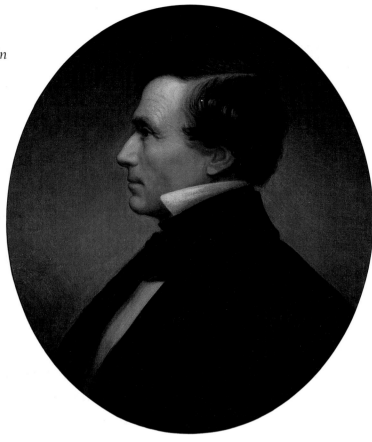

New Hampshire's Franklin Pierce was the fourteenth U.S. president.

candidates. Pierce was elected as a compromise candidate on the forty-ninth ballot. He won the general election and, at age forty-eight, became the youngest president up to that time.

Pierce's personal life was troubled. Two sons died young. A third son was killed in a railway accident before the eyes of Jane Pierce two months before her husband's inauguration. Mrs. Pierce never recovered from the tragedy. For almost two years she remained a recluse in her bedroom. Dressed in black, she came to be known as "the shadow in the White House."

During his administration, Pierce persuaded the Japanese to

open their ports to world trade, and he extended the United States' southwestern border with the Gadsden Purchase. He was also the first president to have a Christmas tree displayed in the White House. It was a vain attempt to lift the spirits of his depressed wife.

President Pierce's support of slavery in the West and other policies that were considered proslavery earned him the hatred of many Northerners. This doomed his chances of winning the Democratic presidential nomination in 1856. He returned to New Hampshire and died in 1869 from the effects of alcoholism.

GOD-LIKE DANIEL

In Stephen Vincent Benét's short story, "The Devil and Daniel Webster," the great orator Daniel Webster wins a court case against the Devil himself in a battle for the soul of a New Hampshire farmer. Webster may never have beat the Devil, but his eloquence in the courtroom and on the floor of the U.S. Senate made him a legend in his own time.

Daniel Webster was born in Franklin in 1782 and became a lawyer at twenty-three. He was elected to the U.S. House of Representatives, first from New Hampshire and then from Massachusetts, where he moved in 1816. He later became a senator and served as secretary of state to three presidents.

Webster was a man of boundless energy. It is said he rose every day between three and four in the morning, fed his cattle, and then worked until 9:00 a.m. "I have finished my day's work," he would say after breakfast, "written all my letters, and now I have nothing to do but enjoy myself."

Try as he might, however, Webster would never enjoy what he most wanted in life—the presidency. He ran unsuccessfully for the Whig Party's presidential nomination in 1836. Many Northerners refused to support him because of his willingness to compromise on slavery with the South. But to Webster, nothing was more important than keeping the United States whole. In his most famous speech in March 1850 he told the Senate, "I wish to speak today, not as a Massachusetts man, nor as a Northern man, but as an American. . . . I speak today for the preservation of the Union."

Daniel Webster has been called New Hampshire's "greatest native son." He served his country as a representative, senator, and secretary of state under three presidents.

THE WOMAN WHO GAVE US THANKSGIVING

If there is one person we have to thank for the Thanksgiving holiday it is Sarah Josepha Hale from Newport, New Hampshire. For thirty-five years she petitioned to make Thanksgiving, which had been celebrated in America since the time of the Pilgrims, a national holiday. President Abraham Lincoln finally agreed to her wishes and made the last Thursday in November Thanksgiving Day in 1863.

But this isn't all Hale accomplished in her long life. For over forty years, she was editor of one of the first women's magazines in America—*Godey's Lady's Book*. The magazine had a major influence on American women's taste and fashion in the 1800s.

Hale was also a firm believer in education for women and promoted the foundation of Vassar College for women in Poughkeepsie, New York. But she may be best remembered as the author of one of the most beloved children's poems, "Mary Had a Little Lamb."

Less than a decade after Webster's death, his precious Union was shattered by the Civil War. It was a conflict he had done everything in his power to prevent. But this was one feat even the "god-like Daniel," as he was known, could not accomplish.

MAKER OF MONUMENTS

Each year two and a half million people visit the Lincoln Memorial. The man who sculpted the colossal statue inside it was Daniel Chester French, who hailed from Exeter.

French worked five and a half years on the famous statue of

Sculptor Daniel Chester French's most famous work is the statue of Abraham Lincoln in the Lincoln Memorial in Washington, D.C. It has been called "one of America's great shrines."

Abraham Lincoln, but when it was finished and in place he realized his work was not done. The bright glare off the memorial's marble floor made Lincoln's face look garish and grotesque. French decided light shining from above was needed to make Lincoln look serious and dignified. It took him six years to perfect the lighting, but once he had, the statue at last looked "Lincolnesque."

French created many other famous sculptures in his lifetime, including *The Minute Man* in Concord, Massachusetts, which commemorates the Revolutionary War battle that took place there. His statue of George Washington on horseback stands proudly in Paris, France.

French's daughter, Margaret French Cresson, followed in his footsteps and was a well-respected sculptor as well.

FIRST AMERICAN IN SPACE

In April 1961 Soviet cosmonaut Yuri Gagarin became the first human in space. Less than a month later astronaut Alan B. Shepard of Derry followed him.

Shepard was a World War II veteran, who later became a navy test pilot. In 1959 he and six other pilots were chosen for the Mercury space program, America's first manned space flights.

Shepard's trip into space was short but earth-shaking. On May 5, 1961, a rocket carried his capsule, *Freedom 7*, 117 miles into space. Less than fifteen minutes later Shepard began to descend to Earth. "Through the periscope I saw the most beautiful sight of the mission," he wrote in his autobiography. "That big orange and white monster [his parachute] blossomed above me beautifully. It

Alan Shepard's fifteen-minute ride into space on May 5, 1961, was the first made by an American astronaut.

told me I was safe, all was well, I had done it, all of us had done it. I was home free."

Shepard's first voyage into space was nearly his last. An inner ear disorder grounded him in 1963, but surgery cured his problem six years later. In 1971 he returned to space as commander of *Apollo 14*, overseeing the third U.S. landing on the moon. First into space, he was the fifth American astronaut on the moon.

Alan Shepard resigned from the space program in 1974 and was a successful businessman in Houston, Texas, until his death in 1998.

Christa McAuliffe, a social studies teacher at Concord High School, died with six other astronauts in the Challenger *tragedy in January 1986.*

TEACHER IN SPACE

"I touch the future—I teach," reads the marker under a tree at Concord High School. It is a tribute to the school's most celebrated teacher whose life ended in unexpected tragedy.

Christa McAuliffe was born in Framingham, Massachusetts, in 1948 but spent the last eight years of her life teaching social studies in Concord, New Hampshire. When the National Aeronautics and Space Administration (NASA) announced it was looking for a person to become the first civilian in space, Christa was one of 11,000 teachers to apply for the job.

She won and trained hard for her flight on the space shuttle *Challenger*. It was to be the tenth trip into space for the *Challenger*, but bad weather and cold temperatures delayed the takeoff several times. On the frigid morning of January 28, 1986, NASA officials gave the go-ahead despite objections from spacecraft engineers. Just seventy-three seconds into the flight, the *Challenger* exploded and broke apart before the horrified eyes of the world. From an altitude of 46,000 feet the cabin fell into the Atlantic Ocean. All seven crew members were killed.

Christa McAuliffe never fulfilled her dream of conquering space, but her dream remains alive for the thousands of people who visit the Christa McAuliffe Planetarium in Concord, which was built in her honor.

HISTORIAN WITH A CAMERA

Among documentary filmmakers, few have equaled the success of Ken Burns of Walpole. When his eleven-hour epic, *The Civil War*, aired in 1990, it became public television's most watched program up to that time.

Burns was born in Brooklyn, New York, on July 29, 1953. His father taught anthropology and was an avid photographer, who introduced both Ken and his brother, Ric, also a documentary film-maker, to the beauty of still photography at an early age. Still images later became a hallmark of their work.

At Hampshire College in Amherst, Massachusetts, Ken Burns met his future wife and collaborator, Amy Stechler. She helped him with his senior year project, a documentary about Massachusetts's Old Sturbridge Village, a re-creation of a typical New England town of the early 1800s. The couple moved to New Hampshire in 1979.

"I'm always drawn to a good story," says filmmaker Ken Burns, whose recent work includes documentaries about the history of baseball and the Lewis and Clark expedition.

Burns's first professional film, about the building of the Brooklyn Bridge, ran only an hour but took four years of painstaking work to make. He also made documentaries on the religious group the Shakers, Louisiana politician Huey Long, and the Statue of Liberty.

The Civil War was five and a half years in the making. Its use of still photographs and readings from letters and journals evoked the past in a fresh and exciting way. It set a new standard for historical documentaries and made Ken Burns a household name.

A POET IN NEW HAMPSHIRE

Many poets have found inspiration in the dramatic landscape of New Hampshire, perhaps none more than John Greenleaf Whittier. Whittier was born in Haverhill, Massachusetts, in 1807, but was a frequent visitor to New Hampshire. The following is part of a poem that depicts New Hampshire's most famous beach.

HAMPTON BEACH

The sunlight flitters keen and bright,
Where, miles away,
Lies stretching to my dazzled sight
A luminous belt, a misty light.
Beyond the dark pine bluffs and wastes of sandy gray.

The tremulous shadow of the Sea!
Against its ground
Of silvery light, rock, hill, and tree,
Still as a picture, clear and free,
With varying outline mark the coast for miles around.

On—on—we tread with loose-flung rein
Our seaward way,
Through dark-green fields and blossoming grain,
Where the wild brier-rose skirts the land,
And bends above our heads the flowering locust spray.

Ha! like a kind hand on my brow
Comes this fresh breeze,
Cooling its dull and feverish glow,
While through my being seems to flow
The breath of a new life, —the healing of the seas!

Why has this filmmaker looked toward American history for so many of his subjects? "My message has always been that history holds the key to the future," says Burns, "that is, by knowing where you have been, you can know where you're going."

A CHILD AT HEART

Tomie dePaola of New London has been one of America's most popular children's book illustrators and writers for more than thirty years. DePaola was born in Meriden, Connecticut, in 1934. As a child, he put on puppet shows for his two sisters. For one sister's birthday, he wrote his first book, about a mermaid, which was never published.

Author and illustrator Tomie dePaola has written many award-winning children's books.

After college, dePaola worked as an artist and designer. The first children's book that he both illustrated and wrote, *The Wonderful Dragon of Timlin*, was published in 1965 and set the standard for his tales of fantasy brought to life by colorful illustrations. In 1976, he won a Caldecott Honor Award for his illustrations of *Streganona*.

Some of his memorable characters, such as the heroine in *Watch Out for the Chicken Feet in Your Soup*, are based on real people—in this case, his Italian grandmother. "I feel that if I don't actually get involved personally with my characters, whether they be human or animal, and find some personal characteristics either of myself or friends in them, they are not 'real,'" he says. "And that is of primary importance to me—that fantasy be 'real,' from the child-in-all-of-us point of view."

6 A GRAND TOUR

The best way to get to know New Hampshire is to travel around it. Don't just visit the cities and larger towns, but poke around in the state's more out-of-the-way places. There are a lot of nooks and crannies in New Hampshire and each one contains a surprise.

SOUTHERN NEW HAMPSHIRE

Since most visitors to the state enter from southern New England, that's how we'll begin our grand tour. Right across the Massachusetts border in North Salem lies one of the state's best-kept secrets—a thirty-acre site of mysterious stone walls and large blocks of stone called monoliths. The site has been named America's Stonehenge because it closely resembles the huge ancient circle of stones in southern England. This Stonehenge is ancient, too. Archaeologists date charcoal found here back to around 2000 B.C. Who erected these strange formations of stone? Adventurous monks from Ireland? Native Americans? Strange aliens from another planet? No one knows, but the mystery attracts 20,000 visitors a year to the site, which is owned, appropriately, by the Stone family.

A little farther west in Rindge lies another famous landmark. The Cathedral of the Pines is a church with no roof in a pine forest that faces Mount Monadnock. In 1957 the U.S. Congress designated it a national memorial to the men and women who had been killed in war.

PLACES TO SEE

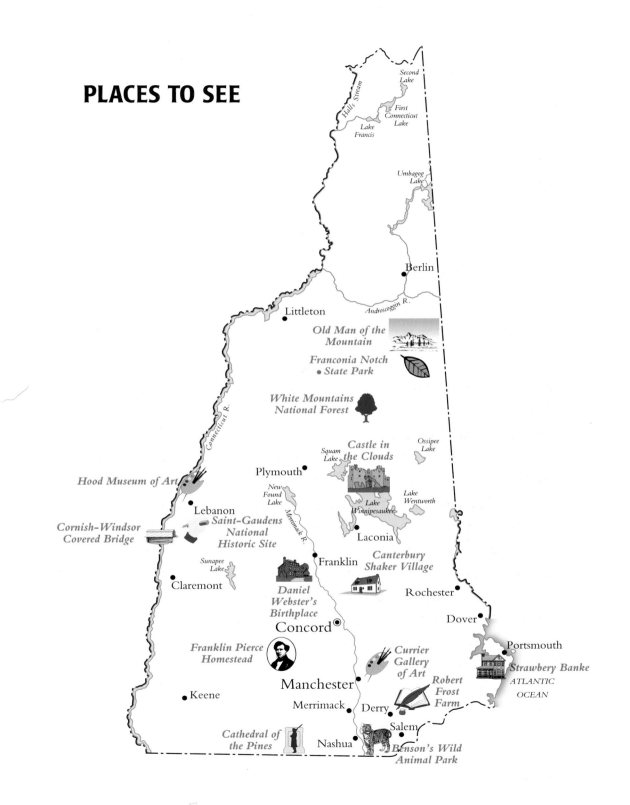

Second Lake

First Connecticut Lake

Hall's Stream

Lake Francis

Umbagog Lake

Berlin

Littleton

Androscoggin R.

Old Man of the Mountain

Franconia Notch State Park

Connecticut R.

White Mountains National Forest

Castle in the Clouds

Squam Lake

Ossipee Lake

Plymouth

New Found Lake

Hood Museum of Art

Lebanon

Saint-Gaudens National Historic Site

Merrimack R.

Lake Winnipesaukee

Lake Wentworth

Cornish-Windsor Covered Bridge

Laconia

Sunapee Lake

Franklin

Canterbury Shaker Village

Claremont

Daniel Webster's Birthplace

Rochester

Dover

Portsmouth

Concord

Franklin Pierce Homestead

Currier Gallery of Art

Strawbery Banke

ATLANTIC OCEAN

Manchester

Robert Frost Farm

Keene

Merrimack

Derry

Salem

Cathedral of the Pines

Nashua

Benson's Wild Animal Park

To the northwest is Keene, home of Keene State College, where many students train to be teachers. Keene's Horatio Colony House Museum is one of the state's most unusual museums. The fine old house, built in 1806, belonged to Horatio Colony, a grandson of Keene's first mayor. In the museum Colony's family heirlooms are displayed alongside exotic souvenirs from his far-flung travels, including several bronze Buddhas.

Heading east again, we come to Nashua, New Hampshire's second-largest town. With more than twenty parks and the fine Nashua Center for the Arts, it has earned a reputation as one of the best places to live in America. Slightly north is Derry, where poet Robert Frost lived for over a decade. His homestead, the Robert Frost Farm, is a popular tourist stop and includes displays on the writer's life and works and a half-mile "poetry nature trail."

A little farther north is Manchester, New Hampshire's largest city, although small by the standard of most eastern states. Once known for its gigantic textile mills, today Manchester is known as much for culture as industry. The Currier Gallery of Art is the state's largest museum and is famous for its collection of decorative art from New England, including silver, pewter, and early New Hampshire–made furniture. It also has one of the largest collections of glass paperweights in the world. Another Manchester site is the childhood home of the longest living general of the American Revolution, John Stark, who died at age ninety-three and is buried in Stark Park.

A short drive north of Manchester is Concord, the state's tiny capital. Visitors who arrive during the legislative session can watch government at work in the capitol. Those with a nose for history can visit Franklin Pierce's house, the Pierce Manse, which is now

This statue in Manchester honors the thousands of young women who worked in the Amoskeag Mills.

TEN LARGEST CITIES

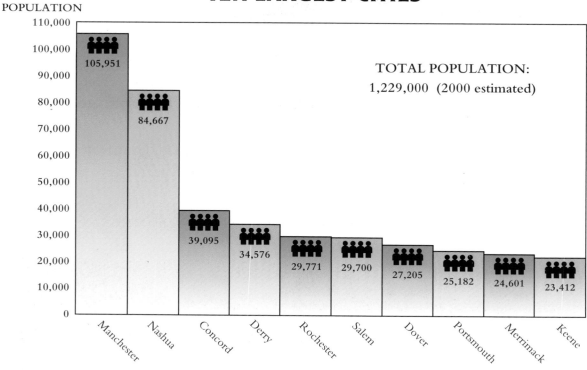

POPULATION

TOTAL POPULATION:
1,229,000 (2000 estimated)

- Manchester — 105,951
- Nashua — 84,667
- Concord — 39,095
- Derry — 34,576
- Rochester — 29,771
- Salem — 29,700
- Dover — 27,205
- Portsmouth — 25,182
- Merrimack — 24,601
- Keene — 23,412

a museum containing the fourteenth president's furnishings and personal memorabilia. Concord is proud of being the home of a U.S. president but is even more proud of New Hampshire's decisive role in ratifying the U.S. Constitution in 1788. A tablet marks the "birthplace of the United States" at the corner of Walker and Boutin Streets.

A little northeast of Concord is Canterbury Shaker Village. The Shakers were a religious sect that came to America from England just before the American Revolution. They got their name from the vigorous dancing that was an important part of their worship service. The Shakers were hard workers and built nineteen communities in the United States. Canterbury was once home to three hundred Shakers; the last died here in 1992. Today, the village is a museum where visitors can tour the buildings that house Shaker-made textiles, furniture, and tools, which are renowned for their simple grace and beauty.

Portsmouth, another historic town, lies to the east, not far from

The Portsmouth Naval Shipyard has been building warships for more than two centuries.

the coastline. The state's second-oldest community, Portsmouth is best known for its naval shipyard, which was established in 1800. Modern submarines are now docked where frigates once were made. John Paul Jones lived here while his warship was being built. The house where he lived is a popular tourist attraction.

Even more impressive is Strawbery Banke, a restoration of a colonial seaport. What makes this ten-acre museum unique is the breadth of history it covers. Visitors can stroll through

The Lowd House, built in 1810, is just one of the many restored historic buildings at Strawbery Banke in Portsmouth.

Lake Winnipesaukee is dotted with many islands.

Portsmouth's past from the seventeenth-century Sherburne House to Abbott's Little Corner Store, which recreates American life during World War II. Strawbery Banke really comes alive at the end of the year, with an annual holiday crafts fair in November and candlelight Christmas strolls in December.

CENTRAL NEW HAMPSHIRE

Central New Hampshire is dominated by Lake Winnipesaukee, the state's largest lake. In the Algonquian language *Winnipesaukee* means "the smile of the Great Spirit." Anyone who has enjoyed

CASTLE IN THE CLOUDS

In Moultonborough, north of Lake Winnipesaukee, is one of the strangest sights in New Hampshire. High atop a mountain is a carved-stone mansion that appears to be floating in the sky. The legendary "Castle in the Clouds" is not a medieval mirage but the dream home of a millionaire shoe manufacturer named Thomas Gustave Plant.

In 1911, Plant hired one thousand Italian masons to carve the stone for his fairy-tale home. Three years and seven million dollars later, it was finished.

The house has sixteen rooms, eight bathrooms, lead doors, and a huge skylight. One secret room, used by Plant for reading, was not entered by another person until after his death in 1941.

Plant's end was not a happy one. He made bad investments and lost all his millions. The house, however, is his legacy, enjoyed by thousands of tourists who visit it each year.

its waters will certainly agree about the smile.

One of the most popular communities on the lakeshore is Wolfeboro, America's oldest summer resort. The town is the site of the Libby Museum, founded by a dentist named Libby in 1912. "When I was forty, life began anew for me," Libby wrote. "It was then that I began to see and feel the force and beauty of Nature. . . . I commenced to collect things." Among Libby's collection are Indian relics and stuffed animals and birds.

Slightly south of Lake Winnipesaukee, at Franklin, is Daniel Webster's birthplace, a two-room frame house. It contains period antiques and artifacts. To the west of Lake Winnipesaukee, near the Vermont border, is Cornish, where the sculptor Augustus Saint-Gaudens created many of his works. At the Saint-Gaudens National Historic Site, you can tour his home, which was originally a country tavern, and his studio. About one hundred of his works are on display. One of Saint-Gaudens's famous sculptures that you won't find here is *Standing Lincoln*, which is in Chicago, Illinois. You can see a model of the impressive work, however.

Nearby is the longest covered bridge still in use in the United States. It crosses the Connecticut River from Cornish into Windsor, Vermont. The 460-foot-long bridge was built in 1866. Until the 1940s, it cost a dime to cross the bridge—now it's free. There are about fifty covered bridges left in New Hampshire, reminders of simpler times.

A little southeast of Cornish is Sunapee, which has been a resort community since the mid-1800s. The word *Sunapee* is Algonquian for "flying geese," which is what you might see on a clear day as you take the popular boat cruise across Lake Sunapee.

Many of Augustus Saint-Gaudens's sculptures are on display at the Saint-Gaudens National Historical Site in Cornish.

The Bath Village Bridge is one of New Hampshire's more than fifty covered bridges.

NORTHERN NEW HAMPSHIRE

For many people, north is the place to go in New Hampshire. Here lie the White Mountains with the great Presidential Range, which includes Mount Washington. The White Mountains National Forest covers much of the mountain region and extends into Maine. It has 1,200 miles of hiking trails, 650 miles of fishing streams, and

A hiker checks out the breathtaking scenery along the Mount Washington Trail.

23 campgrounds. It is the largest wilderness area in New England and the most accessible in the country.

But there are more than the mountains themselves to claim a visitor's attention. The breaks between the mountains are also worth exploring. Writer Harriet Martineau has called Franconia Notch "the noblest mountain pass in the United States . . . [with] its unusual blend of grandeur and grace." A highlight of Franconia Notch is the Flume, a small but spectacular canyon with a series of pools and waterfalls. Another is the Basin, a twenty-foot-wide rock pool with sides polished smooth by eons of sand, stone, and running water.

Crawford Notch separates the Presidential Range from the Franconia Mountains and has some of the roughest terrain in the state. Near Pinkham Notch, Tuckerman Ravine is a skier's dream. It's the only place in the United States east of the Rockies where you can enjoy very steep downhill skiing conditions similar to the kind you'll find in the European Alps.

Bethlehem is a popular resort town for relaxation. Part of its popularity comes from the air, which in summer has a reputation for being nearly pollen free. For years the town was a haven for people suffering from hay fever. It was once the site of the national headquarters of the American Hay Fever Association.

While there are many skiers and tourists in the White Mountains, few residents make their home in this remote region. The largest town in the area is Berlin, with a population of 12,000. It is called the City That Trees Built because its logging industry and paper mills attracted thousands of French Canadians, Russians, and other immigrants decades ago.

THE OLD MAN OF THE MOUNTAIN

His stern visage adorns everything from state highway signs to souvenirs. Many writers have felt compelled to write about him, including Nathaniel Hawthorne, who wrote a story called "The Great Stone Face." To most New Hampshirites he is the Old Man of the Mountain, one of the most familiar rock formations in the country.

His face, forty feet from chin to brow, is formed by five ledges of rock. From his seat atop a cliff on Profile Mountain, he has a clear view of magnificent Franconia Notch.

Daniel Webster described the Old Man this way:

> Men hang out their signs indicative of their respective trades: Shoemakers hang out a gigantic shoe; jewelers, a monster watch; and the dentist hangs out a gold tooth, but up in the mountains of New Hampshire God Almighty had hung out a sign to show that there he makes men.

The old man has inspired many strange legends and tales, including some recent ones. Not long ago, a couple claimed they were abducted by aliens who had landed their flying saucer near the Old Man. It's enough to make the craggy old fellow smile.

A ski jumper zooms through the air at the Gunstock Ski Area in Laconia.

Near Berlin is the 262-foot-high Nansen Ski Jump, once the highest steel tower ski jump in the United States. Berlin is also home to the oldest ski club in America, the Nansen Club, founded in 1872.

Even farther north is tiny Pittsburg, population nine hundred, the state's northernmost town and once the center of the Indian Stream Republic. A farming and lumbering community, Pittsburg is the last rest and supply stop for hunters and fishermen heading north to the remote Connecticut Lakes, which is about as far north as you can go in New Hampshire before bumping into Canada.

From top to bottom, New Hampshire is full of little treasures. You just have to look around for them in the nooks and crannies.

THE FLAG: The state flag is a blue field containing the state seal surrounded by laurel leaves and nine stars which indicate that New Hampshire is the ninth state.

THE SEAL: The state seal depicts the frigate Raleigh in the center, a granite boulder on the left, and a rising sun in the background. Around the scene are the words "Seal of the State of New Hampshire," the date 1776, and a laurel wreath.

STATE SURVEY

Statehood: June 21, 1788

Origin of Name: Named for the English county of Hampshire by Captain John Mason in 1629

Nickname: The Granite State

Capital: Concord

State Motto: Live Free or Die

Bird: Purple finch

Animal: White-tailed deer

Freshwater fish: Brook trout

Saltwater fish: Striped bass

Flower: Purple lilac

Wildflower: Pink lady's slipper

Purple finch

Pink lady's slipper

OLD NEW HAMPSHIRE

New Hampshire has the unusual distinction of having nine state songs. "Old New Hampshire" is the official song and the others are all "honorary." Composed in 1926, "Old New Hampshire" was adopted by the legislature in 1949.

Words by Dr. John F. Holmes

Music by Maurice Hoffman

Tree: White birch

Insect: Ladybug

Amphibian: Red-spotted newt

Gem: Smoky quartz

Rock: Granite

Mineral: Beryl

GEOGRAPHY

Highest Point: 6,288 feet above sea level, at Mount Washington

Lowest Point: Sea level, along the Atlantic coast

Area: 9,279 square miles

Greatest Distance, North to South: 180 miles

Greatest Distance, East to West: 93 miles

Bordering States: The Canadian province of Quebec to the north, Massachusetts to the south, Vermont to the west, Maine to the east

Hottest Recorded Temperature: 106°F at Nashua on July 4, 1911

Coldest Recorded Temperature: -46°F at Pittsburg on January 28, 1925

Average Annual Precipitation: 42 inches

Major Rivers: Androscoggin, Connecticut, Merrimack, Piscataqua, Saco, Salmon Falls

Major Lakes: Mascoma, Newfound, Ossipee, Squam, Sunapee, Umbagog, Winnipesaukee

Trees: beech, birch, elm, fir, maple, oak, pine, spruce

Wild Plants: black-eyed Susan, daisy, fireweed, gentian, goldenrod, purple trillium, violet, wild aster

Animals: beaver, black bear, bobcat, chipmunk, gray squirrel, mink, moose, muskrat, otter, porcupine, raccoon, red fox, red squirrel, skunk, snowshoe hare, white-tailed deer, woodchuck

Snowshoe hare

Birds: blue jay, chickadee, duck, goose, loon, purple finch, robin, sparrow, woodpecker

Fish: bluefish, brook trout, brown trout, bullhead, cod, cunner, cusk, flounder, haddock, hake, lake trout, largemouth bass, mackerel, perch, pickerel, pollock, rainbow trout, salmon, smallmouth bass, striped bass, tuna, whitefish

Endangered Animals: Arctic tern, Atlantic salmon, bald eagle, dwarfwedge

mussel, eastern bluebird, Indiana bat, karner blue butterfly, lynx, osprey, peregrine falcon, pine marten, purple martin, shortnose sturgeon, sunapee trout, whip-poorwill

Endangered Plants: Robbins' cinquefoil, small whorled pogonia

Lynx

TIMELINE

New Hampshire History

1600s The region is occupied by the Western Abenaki Indians

1603 English captain Martin Pring explores mouth of the Piscataqua River, near present-day Portsmouth

1605 French explorer Samuel de Champlain lands at Piscataqua Bay, sails along New Hampshire coast, and discovers Isles of Shoals

1614 Captain John Smith of England sails along Atlantic coast and lands on Isles of Shoals, which he names "Smith's Islands"

1622 Sir Ferdinando Gorges and Captain John Mason granted the land between the Merrimack and Kennebec Rivers (present-day New Hampshire and Maine)

1623 David Thomson founds first settlement, at Odiorne's Point in Little Harbor, now called Rye; Edward Hilton settles Hilton's Point, now Dover

1629 John Mason granted the area between the Merrimack and Piscataqua Rivers; he names it New Hampshire

1638–39 Clergyman John Wheelwright founds Exeter; colonists led by Reverend Stephen Bachiler found Hampton

1641 The four New Hampshire towns place themselves under government of Massachusetts

1679 New Hampshire separates from Massachusetts and becomes a royal province

1692 New Hampshire becomes separate province

1734 A religious revival known as the Great Awakening sweeps through New Hampshire

1756 New Hampshire's first newspaper, the *New Hampshire Gazette*, is established in Portsmouth

1770 Dartmouth College opens at Hanover (formerly known as Moor's Indian Charity School)

1774 Paul Revere rides to New Hampshire to warn of British military buildup in Massachusetts; some 400 colonists capture military supplies from the British at Fort William and Mary in New Castle and supply arms for Battle of Bunker Hill

1775 First Provincial Congress meets at Exeter; Revolutionary War breaks out in Massachusetts, hundreds of New Hampshirites go to fight

1776 New Hampshire becomes the first colony to declare independence, six months before signing Declaration of Independence

1777 Vermont separates from New Hampshire and creates an independent republic

1784 State constitution adopted

1788 New Hampshire is ninth state to ratify United States Constitution

1808 Concord becomes state capital

1819 State capitol completed; religious toleration act prohibits taxation for church purposes

1833 The nation's first free, tax-supported public library founded at Peterborough

1852 New Hampshire native Franklin Pierce elected 14th president of the United States

1917–18 Portsmouth Naval Shipyard becomes important builder of warships during World War I

1961 New Hampshirite Alan Shepard is first U.S. astronaut to travel in space

1963 New Hampshire legalizes lottery, the nation's first since 1894

1986 Concord high school teacher Christa McAuliffe and six others perish as space shuttle *Challenger* explodes soon after liftoff

1988 New Hampshire joins eight other states in a suit to force the Environmental Protection Agency to establish acid-rain controls in Midwest

1990 New Hampshirite David Souter appointed associate justice of U.S. Supreme Court

ECONOMY

Agricultural Products: apples, beef cattle, berries, Christmas trees, eggs, hay, maple syrup, milk, poultry

Manufactured Products: computers, electric lamps, electronics equipment, lumber, metals, paper products, plastics, wood products

Natural Resources: clay, feldspar, forests, granite, gravel, sand

Business and Trade: banking, education, finance, health care, insurance, real estate, tourism

Lumber

CALENDAR OF CELEBRATIONS

Dartmouth Winter Carnival In Hanover every February, elaborate ice sculptures grace the Dartmouth Green. This celebration of winter also includes ski jumping.

Mount Washington Valley Chocolate Festival Earn your chocolate by cross-country skiing from inn to inn, picking up sweets at each stop. This delicious festival takes place in North Conway in February.

World Championship Sled Dog Derby For three days in Laconia in February, you can watch colorful teams of sled dogs race.

Frostbite Follies Sleigh rides, ski races, ski movies, and broom hockey are all included in these follies, which are held in Franconia in February.

Maple Season Tours In Bethlehem during April, you can attend workshops to learn about gathering sap and boiling it down to make maple syrup.

New Hampshire Annual Sheep and Wool Festival This May festival in New Boston includes Border collie demonstrations. Shearing, carding, and spinning are also demonstrated.

Quacktillion and Wildquack River Festival In Jackson Village in May, you can cheer on one of 2,000 rubber ducks as they race down the river; you can even rent your own for $5.

Market Square Days Celebration This lively street fair takes place in Portsmouth in June. It includes music, booths selling food and crafts, and a clambake.

International Children's Festival This June festival in Somersworth has four entertainment stages, including one just for kids, a craft fair, food booths, and a hands-on crafts tent for children.

Revolutionary War Days Each July, Exeter celebrates the Revolutionary War with battle re-enactments, period crafts and antiques, and a visit from George Washington at the American Independence Museum.

League of New Hampshire Craftsmen's Fair Mount Sunapee State Park in Sunapee is the site for this, the nation's oldest crafts fair. The nine-day August gathering includes music, art exhibits, and crafts demonstrations.

Lancaster Fair Every Labor Day weekend, Lancaster hosts this old-fashioned country fair. There are thrill rides, a 4-H animal-judging competition, displays of vegetables and handicrafts, oxen and horse pulling, and harness racing.

Lancaster Fair

Riverfest Celebration For three days every September Manchester comes alive with fireworks, entertainment, and canoe competitions.

World Mud Bowl Each September in North Conway, this annual charity football game is played in knee-deep mud.

Harvest Day This Shaker-style celebration of the harvest in Canterbury each October includes exhibits and games.

Oh! Christmas Tree In Bethlehem each December, you can enjoy wreath making, ornament making, and a hay-wagon tour of a Christmas tree plantation. You can even pick your own tree to cut.

Candlelight Stroll at Strawbery Banke Join carolers for a Christmas stroll in Portsmouth through nine historic homes decorated for the holiday season. More than 1,000 candles light Strawbery Banke's 10-acre grounds.

First Night New Hampshire There are First Night celebrations in Concord,

Keene, Portsmouth, and Wolfeboro. This final night of the year typically starts with a parade and ends with fireworks.

STATE STARS

Josiah Bartlett (1729–1795) was a Revolutionary War patriot and New Hampshire delegate to the Second Continental Congress. Bartlett was the second person to sign the Declaration of Independence. He was also chief justice of the Supreme Court, the first governor of New Hampshire, and a practicing physician for 45 years.

Josiah Bartlett

Amy Marcy Beach (1867–1944), the most prominent American woman composer of her time, was born in Henniker. In 1896, she composed the *Gaelic Symphony*, the first published symphonic work by an American woman. In 1923, she cofounded the Association of American Women Composers.

Amy Marcy Beach

Elizabeth Gardner Bouguereau (1837–1922) was an artist born in Exeter. She was the first woman to exhibit a painting at the Paris Salon of the French Academy of Art and the first woman awarded a Gold Medal by the exclusive academy.

Alice Brown (1856–1948) wrote short stories and plays describing the people and places of New Hampshire, including *Meadow-Grass: Tales of New England* and *Children of Earth*. She was born in Hampton Falls.

Ken Burns (1953–   ) is a famous documentay filmmaker who was born in New York City. After receiving a degree in film studies in 1975, Burns formed his own company, Florentine Films His documentaries include *Baseball*, *Lewis and Clark*, and the 11-hour Emmy-winning *Civil War*. He resides in Walpole.

Benjamin Champney (1817–1907), who was born in New Ipswich, was an artist and one of the founders of the Boston Art Club. After painting landscapes in Europe in the 1840s, he began landscape painting in the White Mountains of New Hampshire. He founded an art colony in the North Conway area.

Benjamin Champney

Charles Anderson Dan (1819–1897) was a journalist and U.S. assistant secretary of war under President Abraham Lincoln. From 1868 to 1897 he was the owner and editor of the *New York Sun*, an influential newspaper. He was born in Hinsdale.

Mary Baker Eddy (1821–1910) was born in Bow, near Concord. During her recovery in 1866 from a severe fall, she turned to the Bible and formulated a spiritual and metaphysical system of healing that became known as Christian Science. Admired for her writings, she founded the *Christian Science Monitor* in 1908, an acclaimed newspaper that has maintained a wide circulation.

Mike Flanagan (1951–   ) pitched for the Baltimore Orioles and the Toronto Blue Jays. In 1979 Flanagan won the Cy Young Award for winning more baseball games than any other pitcher in the American League. He was born in Manchester.

Elizabeth Gurley Flynn (1890–1964), who was born in Concord, was the first woman to head the Communist Party in the United States. She was president of the American Communist Party from 1961 to 1964 and helped factory workers throughout the United States gain more rights and improve working conditions. In 1920 Flynn helped found the American Civil Liberties Union, an organization that works for citizens' rights.

Robert Frost (1874–1963) was a four-time Pulitzer Prize–winning poet who wrote about rural New England. One volume of his poetry is called *New Hampshire*. Frost attended Dartmouth College in Hanover and later lived on farms in Derry and Franconia.

John Irving (1942–   ) is a novelist known for creating eccentric characters. One of his best-known books, *The World According to Garp*, was nomi-

nated for the National Book Award and made into a movie. Another of Irving's books, *The Hotel New Hampshire*, was also made into a movie. Irving was born in Exeter.

John Irving

Kancamagus (1655?–1691?) was the last chief of the Pennacook Indians in New Hampshire. When war broke out between the British and the Indians, Kancamagus led his people to Canada to escape attacks. A highway in New Hampshire following that route is named after him.

Christa McAuliffe (1948–1986), a Concord social studies teacher, was chosen by NASA in 1985 to be the first private citizen and teacher in space. She was killed when the space shuttle *Challenger* exploded over the Atlantic Ocean 73 seconds after liftoff on January 28, 1986.

Bob Montana (1920–1975) created the popular comic strip *Archie* in 1942, which described the lives of American teenagers. Many of the characters were based on classmates from Montana's high school in Manchester.

Franklin Pierce (1804–1869) was the 14th president of the United States. Pierce, the only U.S. chief executive from New Hampshire, was born in Hillsboro.

Charles Alfred Pillsbury (1842–1899) was a flour miller born in Warner. He established a flour mill in Minnesota, which became C.A. Pillsbury and Co., one of the world's largest flour producers in the 1880s.

Eleanor Porter (1868–1920) was a children's author born in Littleton. She wrote *Pollyanna*, a book about a perpetually cheerful little girl, which sold more than a million copies and has been made into several films.

J. D. Salinger (1919–   ) is the author of *Catcher in the Rye*, a classic novel about the problems a teenage boy faces growing up, and many short stories. He lives near Cornish.

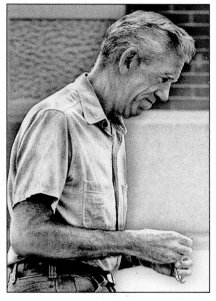

J. D. Salinger

Alan Shepard (1923–1998) was born in East Derry. After serving in World War II, Shepard became a navy test pilot and joined the astronaut program. The first American in space, he orbited the earth in the rocket *Freedom 7* in May 1961. Years later he commanded the third mission to the moon in *Apollo 14* and was the fifth man to walk on the moon.

Earl Silas Tupper (1907–1983) founded Tupperware. He began selling his plastic storage containers to stores in the mid-1940s, but they did not become popular until a decade later when housewives organized home parties to sell them. Tupper was born in Berlin.

Daniel Webster (1782–1852), who was born in Salisbury (now Franklin), was a lawyer, orator, and statesman. He was a U.S. representative, a U.S. senator, and U.S. secretary of state. He is best remembered for his speeches, especially his inspiring words to the Northern soldiers during the Civil War: "Liberty and Union, now and forever, one and inseparable!"

Eleazar Wheelock (1711–1779) was an American educator and Congregationalist minister. He was the founder and first president of Dartmouth College in Hanover.

George Hoyt Whipple (1878–1976) was a pathologist who discovered how to reverse the dangerous effects of a blood disease called anemia, which won him the 1934 Nobel Prize for physiology/medicine. He was born in Ashland.

TOUR THE STATE

Annalee's Doll Museum (Meredith) This museum is home to more than 1,000 flexible felt dolls, 300 of which are on display at any one time. The dolls were created by Annalee Thorndike and are set against a backdrop of dioramas depicting New Hampshire scenes.

Canterbury Shaker Village (Canterbury) This village was founded in 1792 by the Shaker religious sect. Buildings, furniture, and crafts are on display, demonstrating Shaker craftsmanship and design.

Castle in the Clouds (Moultonborough) Visit the castle overlooking Lake

Winnipesaukee built by millionaire Thomas Gustave Plant in 1913. The 5,200-acre estate includes waterfalls, ponds, streams, trails, and great views of the countryside. The castle was built without nails and has doors made of lead.

Cathedral of the Pines (Rindge) This outdoor cathedral is used for nondenominational services. The Memorial Bell Tower, built of local stone, honors American women killed in wars, and the Altar of the Nation recognizes all American war dead. Congress made this shrine a national memorial in 1957.

The Christa McAuliffe Planetarium (Concord) This planetarium, a memorial to the first teacher in space, has the most advanced planetarium projection system in the world. It can simulate space travel up to 600 light-years from Earth and a million years into the future or the past. Look through the 40-foot dome telescope, or check out the tornado tubes, magnetic marbles, and other hands-on exhibits.

*The Christa
McAuliffe
Planetarium*

Conway Scenic Railroad (North Conway) Ride in a big red coach pulled by an old-fashioned locomotive with a steam or diesel engine at this 1874 Victorian railroad station preserved as a museum. Railroad artifacts, lanterns, and old timetables and tickets are on display.

Daniel Webster's Birthplace (Franklin) This small cabin houses replicas of period furnishings along with childhood mementos of Daniel Webster, the legendary lawyer, orator, and statesman.

Franconia Notch State Park (Easton) The famous Old Man of the Mountain rock formation, which looks like the side of an old man's face, can be seen above Profile Lake. The park also features Flume Gorge, an 800-foot chasm with a waterfall, and an 80-passenger aerial tramway at Cannon Mountain that offers great views of the scenery.

Franklin Pierce Homestead (Hillsboro) See the restored 1804 childhood home of the 14th president of the United States. It was designated a national historic landmark in 1961.

Heritage New Hampshire (Glen) Experience a 300-year review of New Hampshire history. There are photographs, dioramas, rides, animation, and period characters, all helping to bring the history of New Hampshire to life. Hear a speech by George Washington or climb aboard a ship traveling from a 17th-century village in England to the New World.

John Paul Jones House (Portsmouth) This was the temporary home of the Revolutionary War hero who made the famous exclamation "I have not yet begun to fight!" Costumes, glassware, guns, portraits, and documents of the late 18th century are on display.

Lake Winnipesaukee (Laconia) The 70 square miles of Lake Winnipesaukee,

New Hampshire's largest lake, provide plenty of opportunity for sight-seeing, boating, fishing, and water sports. On the east side of the lake, at the Wolfeboro Historical Society Museum, you can see an 18th-century home, a 19th-century firehouse, and an 1820 school.

Monadnock State Park (Jaffrey) This park is the home of Mount Monadnock, the most-climbed mountain in North America. You can see six New England states from the top; you can even make out the Boston skyline.

Mount Washington State Park (Crawford Notch) This park includes the Mount Washington Cog Railway, which opened in 1869 and is like a slow roller-coaster ride and moving museum. The track grade to the summit is the second steepest in the world and was the first of its type.

Museum of New Hampshire History (Concord) This museum features exhibits depicting New Hampshire's history, from the Abenaki Indians to the settlers of Portsmouth. There are also a replica of a fire tower with a view of the city and an original Concord Coach, a 19th-century stage-coach.

New England Ski Museum (Franconia) Here you can see a history of skiing in the East, with a collection of ski photos, as well as old trophies, skis and bindings, boots, and ski apparel from the late 1800s.

Old Fort No. 4 (Charlestown) Visit a reconstruction of a stockaded village as it looked during the French and Indian Wars. During the summer, the staff wears costumes, demonstrates early-18th-century crafts, and re-enacts battles.

Ruggles Mine (Grafton) See the mine where production of mica in the United States began back in 1803. An estimated 150 different minerals and gemstones can be found there. Collect some and take them home.

Saint-Gaudens National Historic Site (Cornish) This is the former summer home and studio of the famous sculptor Augustus Saint-Gaudens. The estate includes a barn/studio, an art gallery, and formal gardens. The sculptor's works, as well as sketches and casting molds, are scattered throughout.

Santa's Village (Jefferson) Feed reindeer, browse through the shops, and have a snack at the village eateries. There are rides and live shows daily.

Science Center of New Hampshire (Squam Lake) This 200-acre science center offers woodland and lake excursions, live animal programs, bird-watching, stargazing, and other informative and fun programs. Squam Lake is where the movie *On Golden Pond* was filmed.

Story Land (Glen) Meet Humpty Dumpty and the Three Little Pigs at this theme park. You can also venture on an African safari, ride on a swan boat, and cool off in the park's "sprayground."

Strawbery Banke (Portsmouth) Strawbery Banke, named for the wild strawberries that once grew there, portrays the evolving life of a waterfront neighborhood from the 1690s to the 1950s. The site includes 42 historic buildings on 10 acres.

FUN FACTS

The first potato in the United States was planted at Londonderry Common Field (now Derry) in 1719.

On April 12, 1934, workers at Mount Washington's weather observatory witnessed the most powerful gust of wind ever recorded on land other than during a tornado. The wind speed was measured at 231 miles per hour.

More people have climbed Mount Monadnock than any other mountain in North America; in the entire world only Mount Fuji in Japan has been climbed more times.

The Brattle organ in St. John's Church in Portsmouth is said to be the oldest pipe organ in the United States. It dates back to 1708 and is still played on special occasions.

More than half of the covered bridges in New England are in New Hampshire, including the longest one in the country—the 460-foot Cornish-Windsor Bridge, which crosses the Connecticut River.

FIND OUT MORE

Want to know more about New Hampshire? Check the library or bookstore for these titles:

GENERAL STATE BOOKS

Aylesworth, Thomas G. and Virginia L. Aylesworth. *Northern New England.* New York: Chelsea House, 1996.

Brown, Dottie. *New Hampshire.* Minneapolis: Lerner Publications, 1993.

Thompson, Kathleen. *Portrait of America: New Hampshire.* Austin, TX: Raintree Steck-Vaughn, 1996.

SPECIAL INTEREST BOOKS

Benét, Stephen Vincent. *The Devil and Daniel Webster.* Mankato, MN: Creative Education, 1990.

Billings, Charlene W. *Christa McAuliffe: Pioneer Space Teacher.* Hillside, NJ: Enslow Publishers, 1986.

Casanave, Suki. *Natural Wonders of New Hampshire: A Guide to Parks, Preserves and Wild Places.* Castine, ME: Country Roads Press, 1994.

Marsh, Carole. *Chill Out: Scary New Hampshire Tales Based on Frightening New Hampshire Truths*. Atlanta: Gallopade Publishing Group, 1994.

_____. *New Hampshire History: Surprising Secrets about Our State's Founding Mothers, Fathers & Kids!* Atlanta: Gallopade Publishing Group, 1997.

Simon, Charnan. *Franklin Pierce: Fourteenth President of the United States*. Chicago: Children's Press, 1988.

VIDEOS

New Hampshire's Mountains and Lakes. 30 mins., Site Productions.

New Hampshire Steam Railroads. Total Marketing Services.

INTERNET

The Official New Hampshire Guidebook.
   http://www.visitnh.gov

Access New Hampshire.
   http://www.nh.com

Across New Hampshire Online.
   http://www.across-nh.com

INDEX

Chart, graph, and illustration page numbers are in boldface.